Reincarnation

A Testimonial

MARIE FRIEND

"Let Marie Friend take you by the hand and lead you on an exploration that can offer greater peace and acceptance…. A single lifetime will end but who you really are will be an eternal journey…. begin to see with new eyes that will transform your life into the adventure it was meant to be."

Jacob Nordby: author of *The Creative Cure: How Finding and Feeling your Inner Artist can heal your Life.*

"Marie Friend writes with the voice of authority from personal experiences, giving each word an authentic sense of truth…. She doesn't tell her clients what they want to hear but what they need to know about past relationships, career or situations…. Whether you believe in reincarnation or not, I highly recommend her book for its fascinating stories of past lives and its spiritual guidance."

Lillian Nader: author of *Theep and Thorp: Adventures in Space.*

© Marie Friend 2022

ISBN: 978-1-66783-614-0

eBook ISBN: 978-1-66783-615-7

BOOKS BY MARIE FRIEND

Star.

Dreams, Mirrors of your Soul.

The Church.

FORWARD

I met Marie in 2009 when I was a new producer of a Lifestyle Morning T.V. show in Portland Oregon and was looking for interesting guests. Marie said she was a past-life regression therapist and I was intrigued. I asked her to come to the T.V. station to show me her process so I could see for myself if it could work on live TV.

So, she did a reading for me. Marie says that the past-life she sees in a reading for a client is applicable to the current life and is typically a life lesson from that past life that needs to be learned in the current one. And, everything in the reading that Marie did for me made perfect sense.

In my case Marie saw my life as an American Indian medicine woman living in Oklahoma during the 1500's when Smallpox was raging across the country and wiping out the Native American population. During this past life I not only cared for my own people but the white man who was responsible for bringing this disease to North America. I was heartbroken and sad, but continued to do this work into my old age. I lived to be seventy two years old; which was very old for those times.

After my session, I told Marie that I had always thought I had been a Native American in a past-life. I have always been drawn to that culture and in my youth even had recurring dreams of such a life. On top of that I have been told by a couple of different psychics that my purpose in this life is that of a healer. Marie was spot on.

And, in case you are wondering, Marie's guest appearance on live TV. was so good that when I asked her to come back a few months later my boss gave her an extra segment and asked her to do a live reading for a couple of comedians who were also on the show that day. She was a hit!

Marie is so full of wisdom and sound advice and my reading was so interesting that I wanted my family to have that experience too. So, I booked a session with her for my (now ex) husband and two daughters.

The reading she gave for my former husband and oldest daughter were both interesting, but it was the reading she gave for my youngest daughter that blew me away.

My youngest daughter is one of those kids Marie mentions near the end of this book. According to the reading there are people who chose to come to this planet to help save it from destruction. She says that my youngest daughter is one of them.

I will say that I was a little skeptical when I learned this. It made no sense to me when my daughter went through the rebellious teen years. But, in retrospect, my youngest daughter has always been wise beyond her years. Now that she's a young adult thriving in the world, I can see how it could be true that she came here to help save our world.

Are you a skeptic? Marie knows that the world is full of them. She knows that what she does as a past-life regression therapist seems to be odd and crazy to many people. And, she won't try and convince anyone to believe in reincarnation if they don't want to. That is exactly why she is so endearing and why you should absorb this book. Read it with an open mind and I'll bet you'll come away with a new perspective of what's possible in this world.

Tammy Hernandez

Lifestyle TV. Producer. KATU, Portland OR. Affiliate of ABC.

TABLE OF CONTENTS

INTRODUCTION

How It Began

I had no intention of writing another book. Although the ones that I've already produced have received a moderate amount of success, my writing urge had been fulfilled and it was time for me to sit back and take time to smell the roses. In other words, retirement was long overdue.

But, as you've probably found out for yourself, life isn't always predictable. Let's take Christopher Columbus' journey, for example. Did he set out to discover America? No, but he did anyway. And look at what happened. He took a wrong direction. What would this country be like today if he hadn't goofed up? This event changed the course of this land's history, and I can think of numerous scenarios that may have happened if the outcome hadn't been so unpredictable. But did he really take a wrong direction, or did destiny step in and steer him to where he was supposed to land?

By the time you've finished reading this book, you'll soon find out that our free will isn't always in control. We are "free" up to a certain point, but there is a Universal Law that reins us in when we allow our will-power to go rampant. It's at these times that we usually reap what we've sown. We are allowed to play our earthly games any way we want to, but when we break the rules of the game (or travel in the wrong direction) that Law automatically takes over. It's at that time when we either suffer the consequences of our foolish actions, or if we've merely become confused and don't realize that we're lost, we're led to the right path. Read on and you'll see what I mean.

I'd made a promise to myself that whatever time I have left on this earth, I planned on coasting through it, and writing another book was not part of that plan—then the unexpected happened and my freewill was no longer in charge. My comfortable rocking chair was taken away and life set me on a course that resulted in this book.

It all began with a friend's prediction.

One afternoon, this particular friend was visiting with me, and she happens to be an excellent astrologer. Besides having this asset, she's a generous-hearted individual and I thoroughly enjoy her invigorating company. During a lull in our conversation, I asked her if she would update my astrological chart. Even though my lazy lifestyle suits me and I do as I please, I still enjoy knowing what influence the stars have over my everyday life.

Pulling up my chart on her computer, she said, "You are going to write another book."

"*What?* That's B . . . S . . . !" My reaction was not nice. *Even astrologers can get it wrong.*

A few weeks after this incident took place I was attending a Sunday service at a Spiritualist church and listening to the inspiring talk that was being given by one of the church's mediums. Most churches call such talks, sermons, but the mediums at this particular place don't think of themselves as sermonizers. They are a part of the congregation and they are sharing their thoughts with like-minded folk. Before closing the services, the attendees may be given spontaneous messages that come from the spirit world, using the sensitivity of the mediums as their messengers. Apart from being insightful and helpful, these channeled messages are fun to experience. They are also a strong reminder that there is no such thing as death.

This particular Sunday, I was given a message from my favorite medium—a very gifted and spiritual-minded lady.

She said, "I'm being told to tell you that you're going to write another book."

Dah! What can I say? Just as I was enjoying a pleasant lull in my life and drifting along the river in the sanctity of my boat, I was suddenly tipped over and plunged into that shockingly cold water!

Skeptics would probably say that this book was written because the idea was planted in my head—not once, but twice. My answer to the skeptics is this: like Einstein, I believe that time is a man-made concept. In the universe there is no such thing as time. Therefore was this book already written before I was told what to do?

Marie

CHAPTER 1

"They regain the knowledge acquired in former lives and strive even more for perfection. Previous practice alone impels those on the path, striving earnestly; pure from taint they gradually gain perfection and reach the highest goal." ~ Bhagavad Gita

Dear Reader

Thank you for allowing me to come into your life and permitting me to share some of its mysteries with you. This is an invitation to join me in visiting another dimension beyond your five senses; to explore beyond the limitations of your known world. Whether you already believe in reincarnation, or are being introduced to the concept with this book, is not important. What is important is that you've picked it up to read. Either consciously or unconsciously, you've decided to expand your view of life and look outside the boundaries of your earthly existence. You are about to explore the unlimited power of the universe. I'm asking you to come along with me on an adventure into another world, and just like Alice after she fell down that rabbit hole, you'll enter a whole new dimension far from your physical reality.

For a moment, I want you to think of life as being like a series of significant doors that you have your own keys to unlock, allowing you to explore the rooms on the other side. Each door will lead you into a room that is full of new experiences that can either enhance your spiritual growth or cause you to pause and take stock of your life's journey. But, when a door is presented to you, it's always your choice to either walk away or open that door and examine the room within. You can choose to take advantage of those moments that may change your life or not. You do have free will, after all. Yet, unbeknownst to us, if we're reluctant to unlock a door at a certain moment in time, and if it's meant to be, it will spontaneously present itself again when we are ready to go inside. I'm making this statement because from my own experiences, that's a fact.

We think we're in control of our lives, but we're really not. Although the decisions we make are arrived at via free will, what we don't realize is that regardless of the choice we've made, whether it's right or wrong, we will eventually be led to the path we are supposed to be taking. It may be a different door that we're presented with, but the room (experience) and its furnishings on the other side of that door will be the same. In other words, if we miss an opportunity to expand our spiritual development, we'll be given another chance to do so. Sub-consciously we know this and act accordingly.

Of course, I can just hear you saying, "I would never have chosen to do such-and-such in my life if I'd known this was going to happen." Yes, you did! Because you have free will, you sometimes make a poor choice. You enter a doorway that should have remained shut. So, you may ask, how do we know the difference between entrances we're meant to go through and those we should avoid? Listen to your gut instinct. It will warn you with that certain small whisper of nagging doubt if you take heed. Do you know, my friend, that when you experience a gut feeling that it's your third chakra activating? Ah yes, it's like an electrical surge shooting along a wire. The third chakra ties the lower, earth-bound chakras to the upper chakras that connect you with your Higher Self. It is what I refer to as the balancing chakra. Hence, if you are about to make a wrong decision, your gut feelings will raise red flags that you can either take notice of or ignore. Your guardian angels will warn you in whatever way they can, but even the heavens can't interfere with your free will, and if you choose to ignore the warning, so be it. For example, say that still, small voice inside tells you to avoid entering into a relationship with a certain person because their track record with the opposite sex stinks. What do you normally do? You say to yourself, "He (or she) loves me and would never treat me that way." Unfortunately (or fortunately, depending on your perspective), we often learn more from our mistakes than we do when we seem to be making wise decisions. Sad to say, pain is our greatest teacher, and sometimes it takes a painful experience to teach the lesson we're meant to learn.

Do you know that before you are born, you've already decided what you are going to accomplish? That's a given. Regardless of your free will choices, you are still going to do what you came here to do. You may choose a more difficult road than one that is easier to travel in order to get to your destination, but eventually you will get to that pre-ordained goal. Many years ago, I attended one of those non-denominational New Thought churches. The minister was a very good orator and made a statement that resonated with my own beliefs. She said:

> "Before we are born, we make a contract with ourselves and our Divinity. We are going to accomplish this—and this—and --- this—and it's going to be a piece of cake. Then we are born, and what happens? We've forgotten what we came here to do!"

I remember thinking, *you are so right up to a point, but our Soul has not forgotten.*

For the last quarter of a century, I've had the privilege to observe and experience peoples' former lives. In addition, I realize that this gift has allowed me more than my share of relationships, no matter how fleeting and I feel honored to have been given such a privilege. But most important of all is the fact that I've been allowed to have a glimpse of what lies beyond that invisible veil between the limitations of our life as we know it, and the never-ending life of the universe. Over and over again, I've received validation that spirit is eternal and our lives are a continuous story that is divided into individual chapters. It's called reincarnation.

For one moment, think about the life you are leading and the people in it. Life is all about relationships, and I'll get into that subject more thoroughly after I've set the groundwork for you. The reason we incarnate as humans is so we can to have the opportunity to grow spiritually via our interactions with other people. When we get down to the facts of life, relationships are what make our world go around, and depending on the karma that we may have created, those relationships are either smooth sailing or stormy. For example, it may be that relationship with family - close friend - or a special teacher. Or, it could be a relationship on a larger scale between countries. The latter is always a biggie as it has a major effect on the operation of our world. A good example of a karmic relationship between countries is the present one between Hong Kong and China. Would the power struggle between these two pieces of land be so traumatic if England had not returned control of Hong Kong to China? Would this relationship between these two countries be less dramatic if their ideologies had not clashed? Life is what we make it via our interactions with each other. It's commonly known as cause and effect, and history is full of such karmic conditions between countries as well as people. Think about this scenario—what would life in this country be like if America had not won the War of Independence?

Thank goodness that in this life I chose the path I've taken because those one-on-one connections with clients who have sought me out have given me the opportunity to help my fellow man. Helping each other through life should be our number one intention. Have you seen that TV advert that advocates passing it forward? It's one of the few commercials that I think needs to be absorbed. We're all together in the same boat, my friend, and we all have to be rowing in sync with each other to get to where we're going because every individual is a part of the Whole. Regardless of what religious and/or spiritual path you choose to travel, we all eventually end up at the same place.

Many folks have tagged me with the title of psychic, but what is a psychic? To be classified as such makes me feel uncomfortable because I'm no different from you. The only thing I've done that might be different from you is to have opened up and utilized my sub-conscious mind. My thinking includes the daily and deliberate use of unconscious as well as conscious thoughts and actions. A simple example of this thought process is that of driving my car on the busy highways. Before taking off, I not only mentally envision a safety net around me but also tune in to the actions of other drivers. By doing this, I instinctively know that the car travelling in the lane alongside mine is going to switch lanes and get in front of me, even if the driver doesn't turn on their signaling device.

Psychiatrists claim that we only use a small amount of our brain capacity. They also claim that we don't know how the unused part works. I'm no psychiatrist, but from my experiences, I'm convinced that this unknown part is where our sub-conscious stores every memory from the day we were born. And it doesn't stop with our birth because it also retains memories of our past lives. Using the sub-conscious part of the brain isn't unique to so-called psychics. Everyone has the capacity to use that section of their brain. Yes, dear reader, that means you. All you need is an implicit belief that you can. I'll take that statement one step further. If people used their sub-conscious minds in their daily actions, they might avoid many of the pitfalls they normally run into. Believe me, if you weren't meant to use it, you wouldn't have it!

I'm convinced that there was a time in human history when we automatically used every single part of our brain. But after becoming "civilized" (I use that word loosely), we forgot how to use the sub-conscious. It's been lying dormant for millennia, waiting to be reactivated. I'll give you an instance whereby you'll see this to be a fact, by sharing an account with you from my own life.

Before I do this however, I need to explain the kind of validations I've personally received regarding my own past lives. Many people have asked if I'm able to see my own previous incarnations. I do, but not in such detail as when seeing someone else's, and only when my Head Honchos (the name

I've given to my guardian angels) feel that it's necessary. I call these incidents "Flash Cards" because all I'm given are short flashes of insight. Because I need to figure out my own lessons, seeing the answers in their entirety would be too easy. It would be like cheating on an exam in school. I may have snatched the answer from someone else's paper, but because I haven't done the necessary homework, I don't know how I arrived at the correct answer and I'm sure this is why I don't see a full picture.

Seeing a completed past life of my own has only happened once, and that wasn't instigated by me. But that's another story I'll talk about later.

Anyway, getting back to how I know that we once used all of our brain's capacities, the following is definitive proof. Many years ago, one of my Flash Cards showed me a life from millions of years ago. It was a life on the lost continent of Lemuria. If you don't know anything about this continent, it's the Pacific Ocean's equivalent of Atlantis. I've never been too curious about Atlantis, but at the time that this brief vision was given to me, I'd been reading a book about this lost continent that's supposedly under the Atlantic Ocean. One day while driving my car, I was thinking to myself, *I wonder if I ever lived in Atlantis.* A mental answer came to me as clearly as if someone were sitting in the passenger seat and talking to me: "You lived in Atlantis, but you loved in Lemuria."

Well, I was dumbstruck! At this point, I knew tiddily poop about this continent that supposedly lies underneath the Pacific Ocean, and even my knowledge concerning that Atlantian continent was puny. After this enigmatic answer, a Flash Card vision appeared as a picture postcard in my mind's eye. I saw the continent of Lemuria, unspoiled by mankind. I saw what is considered a Neanderthal, standing almost seven feet tall with a hairy torso and a high, sloping forehead. The amazing thing was that this ape-like creature was communicating via mental telepathy with another person who was a hundred miles away from him. It surprised me to learn that this early human was so much more mentally alert than we are today. Then my sub-conscious let me see what the civilizations of Lemuria and Atlantis were like at that time. Each one had its own specialty: Atlantis was the home of the scientists—highly intelligent, a materially motivated race with great ambitions, whereas Lemurians were nature lovers—commune dwellers with more of a spiritualistic mindset, although still as intelligent as their Atlantian counterparts. Lemurians kept to themselves and didn't welcome intruders.

My sub-consciousness told me that this Neanderthal I was observing was me in a Lemurian lifetime. And my envious thought was, *Boy! Would I like to have that brain now!* From this brief insight, I believe there was a time when we did use all of our brain capacity and is the reason for my conviction that everyone is still capable of tapping into that unused section.

Why I'd been given this Flash Card I haven't a clue, except maybe it was showing me that I'd used that sub-conscious part of the brain to assist people in this ancient lifetime. Maybe I used it in a healing capacity, which is the reason why it was so easy for me to use it again.

Naturally, I can hear the skeptics thinking, "She's bonkers!" Some professionals who have studied ancient humankind might shake their heads in disbelief, but one thing is certain, this experience proved to me that we've been incarnating since time immemorial, and although our conscious selves may have forgotten, our sub-conscious has not.

And so my friend, with this book I intend to share with you my experiences that have shown me other realities so you too may gain a new level of understanding. I want you to have evidential proof that your life's horizon does not end within the limits of your currently known world.

I'm now at the tail end of this lifetime and in looking back at everything that has happened to me, I'm aware that whether I've made the right decision or the wrong one, everything has eventually taken place as was intended. Sometimes my choice of a road has been heavy duty while sometimes it's been a breeze. It makes no difference as I know it's worked out as planned. We are all given many opportunities to reach our destination, but it takes some of us longer to get there. It depends on whether you take the chance offered to you right away or decide to stay where you are for a longer time. The choice is yours.

If the knowledge that I'm about to share with you allows you to think outside the box just a wee bit, then this book will have served its purpose. Of course, you may already be following New Thought ideas instead of fundamentalist religion, but even nondenominational organizations can box you in if you're not careful. I used to give public talks on réincarnation, and I always gave the participants one piece of advice that I'll now give to you: retain anything I say that feels right for you and discard the rest. This advice applies to anything you are told—or anything you read. Even the Bible has many interpretations and it's probably the reason for so many different religious denominations. And the Bible is only geared toward Judaism and Christianity, so if you think about all the religious beliefs that are in the world, it can be confusing.

Each person has their own concept of truth, and it doesn't mean that someone who has a different opinion from you is wrong and you are right. It's always based on an individual's perception, and he or she is always their own judge.

No matter what a person's religious or spiritual belief system is, or even if they have none at all, we all have one thing in common. Everyone is born, and everyone dies. What happens to us after our physical death, nobody really knows. I happen to believe that we return again and again with the intent of perfecting our spirit so that we can eventually connect to our Divinity.

And, I don't make this statement on faith alone. I've had proof of reincarnation and will share this proof with you.

For one minute, I'd like you to close your eyes and visualize the following. Think of life as a sparkling diamond flashing its brilliant light and dazzling all that see it. Can you see its magnificence? Its sparkle is as bright as the star of Venus. That diamond is you, my friend.

A diamond is made up of carats, and each carat makes up its weight. Some lives may contain so many carats they look like the Hope Diamond. In other words, they are the kind of people who go through life spreading goodwill and positive energy, like the Dalai Lamas, Mother Teresa's or Martin Luther King's of this world. These people display their weight with their influence. Others are so small their facets are indistinguishable and their light hardly noticeable, like that homeless person begging on a street corner or the janitor who cleans office floors. It doesn't matter how big or small a person is in the world, they are still a part of that exquisite diamond we call humanity. If we all remembered that we are indisputably connected to each other while walking our personal paths, wouldn't life be so much easier and non-judgmental?

We need to constantly remember that we are spirit having a human experience and act from spirit first. We are not an important body (ego) that happens to have an unseen spirit. I used to have a bumper sticker on the back of my car that read, "Don't drive any faster than your angels can fly." You'd be amazed at the number of tailgaters who would back off when they were riding my bumper and were dangerously close enough to read that sign. All of us should wear a bumper sticker to remind us to treat others as we would want to be treated ourselves.

Over many years, hundreds of people have come to me to get answers to their problems and try to find their right road through life. Some of these people have sought my help in trying to figure out why their life is so stuck. By placing their trust in me and allowing me to enter their psyche, I've seen a particular past they've lived that shows why they've created the situation they are in now. Other past scenarios have brought validations for a person—they are doing exactly what they are supposed to be doing. We have many past lives, but when I am given a view of a client's past, it is always a life that tells them why they have returned at this present time.

Some folks have asked me if I've ever seen any famous figures in a past life encounter. It's been rare that I've seen someone well known, but it has happened. Keep in mind that we can't all have been Cleopatra or Mark Antony in a previous lifetime! I've read that the country singer Loretta Lynn believes she was Minnehaha in a previous Native American existence. General G. Patton was convinced that he'd been a soldier many times over. It's been said that we all have fifteen minutes of fame and for whatever reason, some folks seem to get more than fifteen minutes. So be it. The bottom line is, regardless of having lived a life of fame, these folks have the same hang-ups as you and me. That is why they were led to see me, not because they were once famous but because they needed help in resolving issues within their present existence.

Some of the past lives that have appeared to me have been funny, some tragic, many mundane, and many magnificent, but all of them have had one thing in common—the person's story from that former life is like that book you haven't had time to finish. Now, the story is being continued in this present lifetime. It bears repeating because it's important to know that it's just another chapter in the continuing story of your spiritual development. Many folks have returned again and again to re-enact the same play. It's a natural law that a person returns either to experience the rewards they've earned, or work on mistakes that they've created in a former life. It's as if you flunked a grade in school and have to repeat that grade. If you don't get it right the first time, you'll do it over again. On the other hand, you may work diligently at the lessons, skip a grade, and move on to a higher level. But from my experiences, I know that there is always a balance to life. A person is never given more than they can bite off and chew. In other words, they are given gifts or talents to help in counteracting their mistakes.

There is more to reincarnation; however, than just creating karma in one life and having to return to undo that wrong we've created in a previous incarnation. The universe doesn't miss the tiniest detail when it comes to guiding your life. Believe me, by the time you've finished reading this book, you'll know what I mean by this last statement. There's so much psychology attached to reincarnation that even a psychologist would have to work overtime at deciphering it all. The main thing is that when you've finished your read, you will have expanded your thoughts regarding some of life's puzzles as they relate to your own life.

To set the groundwork and understand why you need to experience every detail of life, I'll begin with the story of my own journey and how I was led, albeit reluctantly, into believing that reincarnation is a fact. But I need to emphasize that the reason for this groundwork is not coming from the ego. It's because I'm a "show me" person and always need tangible proof of anything unseen, even reincarnation. I feel very strongly about this, and so accordingly, I know that you too deserve to be given the same consideration. I envy those people who have the faith to believe without needing physical proof. That's not me. And so, because of this quirk of mine, I'm not going to ask you to take what I say on faith.

The many facets of reincarnation are just that—fascinating. I've even found that some people are here in this life to take a vacation and enjoy a well-deserved rest, but I'll talk about that another time. Believe it or not, I didn't always believe in reincarnation and spent half of my life pretty ignorant of all its intricacies.

I'm now about to share a few of these life stories with you that will validate all the reasons as to why we keep on returning. My expectation is that these ordinary past life revelations will give you the understanding that you need to allow past life wisdom to help you. If you are at a point in your life where you're searching for a new direction, or if you are just curious to learn more about reincarnation, you've come to the right place, or more accurately, found the right book.

CHAPTER 2

The Dream Workshop

It started at the beginning of the 1970s. I'm talking about my belief in reincarnation, or to be more accurate, my first introduction to it.

But, before I get any further into this account, I need to emphasize one fact. The God Force in whatever form you believe your Divinity to be doesn't mess around when it comes to directing our lives. If we're playing hide-and-seek, we are going to be found whether we're ready or not. At this time in life, I didn't realize that I was hiding from myself and certainly was not ready to be invaded by such nonsense!

Looking back to those years, I cringe at that ignorant and opinionated person that I was. My life was uneventful, and seeking anything beyond daily existence wasn't on my agenda. Regardless, my Head Honchos didn't let this attitude faze them. I was as green as grass when it came to the subject of reincarnation and didn't know the first thing about it. Fortunately, I've always been open to learning something new in general, and I was now about to take that first baby-step toward a life that, to say the least, has proven to be an unusual adventure. The following account is an illustration of being offered a key to a particular door and ignoring the chance to use it and explore unlimited horizons.

• • • • ● ● ● • •

Exasperation showed in my voice that day. "What are you trying to drag me into now?"

My best friend chuckled as she took note of the skeptical expression on my face. "Come on! You're always talking about how serious you are about your dreams, aren't you? I thought you would jump at the chance to share them with like-minded people."

She was right as far as taking my dreams seriously. Apart from having had precognitive dreams for as far back as I could remember, I grew up in a family where anything paranormal was considered perfectly normal. Luckily for me, as it later turned out, I'd had a mother who came from a very weird family background. My maternal great-grandmother had been a Welsh gypsy. And although I'd never known her daughter (my maternal grandmother) as she'd died when mother was only ten years old, I had grown up around some of this grandparent's siblings with their spooky minds. The result was that at an early age, my mother, who had inherited their spookiness, encouraged me in the same paranormal thinking. For example, at an early age and along with these gypsy relatives, she would take me to spiritualistic meetings where mediums brought messages for people from departed entities. These relatives also introduced me to lots of other abnormal events that impacted my childish mind and I soaked it all up like a sponge. My mother also had a lot of extra-sensory perception that I automatically accepted and took in stride. Instead of discrediting my dreams, she would help me to interpret their messages. She even went as far as to teach me how to read tea leaves. Such was my childhood environment.

So, I'd grown into adulthood believing that everyone accepted paranormal stuff, especially precognitive dreams. I only learned of my mistake about others' perceptions when I'd discuss a dream with someone, and they'd look at me as if I needed a shrink. Needless to say, I no longer shared them with just anyone. I'd become more selective and my friend Fran was one of those few exceptions. Anyway, when she told me of this so-called dream workshop and wanted me to join her in attending their meeting, I was skeptical. Knowing nothing about it and having learned to be selective about sharing my dream experiences, I felt reluctant to listen to her persuasions.

After divorcing my children's father, I'd moved as far away as possible from him. All I'd wanted was a peaceful existence after a far from peaceful marriage, and a good job offer in Phoenix, Arizona, had appealed to me. Fran and I had met via our mutual fourteen-year-old daughters who had bonded in the school in which I'd registered my children. As it happened, they lived a few houses from my new home. Fran was also a divorcée, and her four children were the same ages as mine. Although we hadn't known each other very long, there was an instant connection between us, and even though I soon found out what an impulsive creature she was, she was fun to be around. Her outgoing Gemini personality seemed to complement the down-to-earth Capricorn in me. We suited each other.

I gave an inward sigh, knowing that she wasn't about to give up on her latest plan. "Who told you about this dream workshop?" I asked.

"A girl at work. It sounded like such fun that I asked her where it was being held. She's been there before, and apparently it's held every month at a place called the Edgar Cayce Clinic that's located somewhere downtown."

Edgar Cayce clinic? I tried to wrap my mind around this information. "I've never heard of the place," I declared. "But I have heard something about this Edgar Cayce character. Wasn't he some sort of psychic who ran a healing place somewhere on the East Coast?"

"Yes, but this clinic is an offshoot of that other place. The original is in Virginia, I think. The clinic here is used for some kind of natural healing modalities, among other things. At least, that's what this co-worker told me."

She sounded vague, and I suspected that despite her enthusiasm, my friend knew next to nothing about this so-called dream workshop. *At least, she seems to know more than I do.* I have to admit she'd finally gained my attention as I never could resist anything to do with dreams. It sounded like it might be fun. *What do I have to lose?*

I made up my mind. "Okay, lady, so when will the next meeting take place, and what time does it start?"

Giving a jubilant grin, she answered, "Tonight at seven-thirty."

● ● ● ● ● ● ● ●

The building looked like many of the other businesses in this downtown section of Phoenix. Only the announcement board displayed outside its entrance gave away its purpose. It advertised the place as the A.R.E (Association for Research and Enlightenment) Clinic and gave a list of names with medical-sounding titles at the end of each entry. After entering the front door, we found ourselves in the standard business office lobby with a directory hanging on a wall that faced the door. However, the directory was unnecessary as a large placard sitting on a stand stated that the dream workshop was being held in the library. Underneath the word "library" was a red arrow pointing in the direction of a long hallway that veered off the lobby's right hand wall.

Immediately on entering the room, a distinctive, musty smell of printed matter hit me. It was that same smell that most libraries seem to have and with good reason, since it was full of floor-to-ceiling bookshelves lined up like soldiers on parade. Metal book racks took up empty spaces between the library's shelves, and narrow walkways were the only empty spots left among all the bookshelves and racks. As I scoured the large room, my eyes came to rest on one far corner. A space was wide open and held a circle of chairs in which a few people were seated. Obviously this was the dream group we were here to join. We made our way toward the circle and I gave brief glances at the book racks that we passed, noticing that most of the books' titles told me that they were all of a metaphysical nature. Many of the books seemed to be stories about the psychic known as Edgar Cayce.

Four women and a couple of men were seated in the circle, and they smiled with nods of greeting as we chose two empty seats and sat down. We smiled back but remained silent. It seemed like silence was expected. It didn't take very long before other people began to wander in and the other chairs started to fill. Eventually, a tall, slim woman of indeterminate age and with a look of authority entered the circle. She sat down and it soon became obvious from her demeanor and the expectant expressions on the people's faces in the circle that she was to lead the meeting.

"Let's start by going around and introducing ourselves. I'm Ellie," she said. Turning to the person sitting to her left, she nodded, and the introductions carried on around the group.

It was my turn and Ellie addressed me. "You're new here, aren't you?" She nodded at Fran sitting next to me, and then turned her attention back to me. With a smile of encouragement, she said, "Welcome to both of you."

So far, it didn't seem too bad and I felt comfortable, looking forward to this event with a sense of expectation.

One by one, folks began to relate dreams that they'd had, and then other people in the group would volunteer their interpretations of that person's dream. *This is right up my alley!* I thought as I listened to the variety of dreams and an even larger variety of interpretations from the participants. The majority of them were surprisingly good, and I was enjoying this meeting of like-minded folks. It seemed I'd found people who didn't think dreams were a bunch of baloney, and I felt as if a breath of fresh air had blown my way.

Now it was my turn to share.

The previous night I'd had one of the strangest dreams ever, and it had been so stark and real that unlike most dreams that fade on awakening, I had remembered every detail. As I'd gone through the day at my job, the dream had stuck at the back of my mind. Now, I was eager to share it with these people. *What will they make of it?* I started to relate my dream:

—————

17

I was walking down a cobblestone country lane, and my mother was following behind. All at once I felt cold chills surge through my body as if an icy blast of wind had hit me. I stopped walking and stood still, but suddenly my body started to vibrate like a spinning top. In spite of the chilling gust and whirling sensation, I felt no fear, only surprise. It didn't last long, and when it stopped I turned around, expecting to see my mother standing behind me. She'd gone. Instead, I saw a young woman dressed in the fashion of the Victorian era. Her pale face peeked out from the wide brim of a pink bonnet with silk ribbons tied in a bow beneath her chin. Her hooped dress was the same shade as her bonnet. Dark brown eyes stared straight at me, and I felt like I knew her from someplace but couldn't remember where we'd met. Thick black ringlets framed her face and the phrase, "This is the lady of the manor," entered my head. As fast as she'd appeared, she was gone, and the dream ended.

I stopped talking and looked questioningly at the other people, expecting some responses.

Everyone remained silent. No one stirred.

Finally, the leader spoke. "You were not dreaming. You were experiencing a past life."

What! I'm sure my mouth dropped open, but before I could respond, Ellie continued: "Your Mother represented the generation before yours and the Victorian lady was you in that former life." I couldn't believe my ears but she didn't stop. "Whenever you go back into a former life, your body vibrates as if you're in a whirlwind," she explained. "This is what happened to you."

The rest of the people still didn't say anything, but there were several murmurs of agreement and the nodding of heads.

I was dumb-struck. *Reincarnation? What an absolute bunch of garbage!* Even taking into consideration that my family upbringing was more eccentric than most, the subject of reincarnation had never entered any discussions among my mother's relatives. I doubt that anyone of them, even as cuckoo as they were, had ever given any thought to reincarnation. Throughout my whole life, I'd never given it any thought—until now. *What utter rubbish!*

I stared at Ellie and answered with the first thought that popped into my head. With an arrogant toss of my head I said, "If I thought I'd have to come back and marry my ex-husband again, I'd kill myself right now!"

The atmosphere turned as chilly as that wind-blast I'd encountered. Ellie straightened up and appeared to grow taller in her seat. She didn't look one bit amused. Leaning toward me, she looked me right in the eye and said, "Young lady if you don't change your attitude, you WILL come back and do it all over again!"

I felt like an idiot.

As I didn't know the slightest thing about reincarnation, it never entered my supercilious mind that if I did kill myself, I'd return with a lot more baggage to work through!

Aftermath

As I now share this event with you dear reader, I'm thinking to myself, *you've come a long way, baby!*

What a foolish and arrogant young woman I must have seemed to be to that group of spiritually advanced individuals. I was blind to the fact that my Head Honchos had opened a door for me to go through and I'd slammed it shut. I wasn't ready to enter this new dimension that would lead me on the right path.

My friend, take heed. Make sure that you don't make the same mistake as I did. My suggestion to you is that when you're presented with an opportunity to expand your spiritual horizons, don't hesitate any longer than it takes to blink an eye, even if the situation seems bizarre to you. Just because you are ignorant of the subject doesn't mean that it's wrong. Don't be judgmental until you've checked the situation out and gathered more information.

———

Today, as I now share that incident with you, it seems as if I'm remembering someone else and not me. That person no longer exists.

As my life is now, I know that display of sarcasm I'd shown was ludicrous and also rude. The only excuse I can make is that I wasn't ready to take that particular leap. At that time I hadn't really known who Edgar Cayce was, and yet I had sat in a library surrounded by every book that had ever been written about his life and work. What an amazing opportunity had been presented to me and I'd ignored it! As for my reaction to the interpretation of that dream, well I still cringe at the memory of the crass answer I'd given. But the most important lesson that I learned from that experience is that there are no such things as accidents. I was meant to attend that dream group, but how I reacted to the insights I received depended entirely on me. And I goofed up. Yet, every mistake that you make in your life is only a longer road you've decided to travel, instead of taking the highway that will get you to your destination faster. Yes, even your mistakes aren't wasted. We all learn and grow via negative actions as well as those that are positive. Even though I wasn't ready to go through that door at that particular time, the seed was definitely planted. Without realizing it, I was being prepared for a life that has proven to be extraordinary and fulfilling. Even with its ups and downs, it's still been a soul searching adventure.

This is what happens to everyone, even you my friend. You might miss that exit ramp off the highway that you were supposed to take to get to your destination, but you'll always be guided back to the road you're meant to travel, even if you've gone a few miles out of your way. Just make sure you don't run out of gas before you get there! Close a door that you are meant to enter, and it will spontaneously re-open for you when you are ready to go through it. Be prepared to enter and explore that which is beyond.

Incidentally, there's an interesting closure to my dream of that former life, but that's another story to tell. Meanwhile, the dream did prompt a memory from my childhood to resurface and once more, impacted my psyche.

I don't remember exactly when my mother had told me the story of my father's ancestry, but it seems to have been handed down as a part of his family heritage. According to my mother, my dad's grandmother (my paternal great-grandmother) had been an illegitimate child. She had never known who her mother was. I personally never knew this relative because she died long before I was born, but her life story is intriguing.

Apparently, she was raised by a foster woman who lived in an English country village. She remembered that as a child, she'd always had nice clothes and had worn shoes every day. It's a known fact that in Victorian times, poor children usually went barefoot except on special occasions, such as going to church on Sundays. Her foster mother was a working-class peasant and would not have been able to afford such clothing. Until around age seven, this paternal ancestor remembered frequent visits by two women who rode on horses. After this great grandparent reached an age where she became more aware of people in her life, she asked the peasant woman who these visitors were. The woman didn't answer the child's query, but the two women stopped visiting. The surrogate mother made no secret of the fact that the child was not her own but never revealed the identity of her birth mother. When this woman was dying, my great-grandmother begged her to tell who her mother was, but the old lady refused to do so.

Doesn't it sound like a sensational item out of the National Enquirer? That's what I always thought; especially as my mother's romantic ideas came into play. She was convinced that my father's grandmother had been the illegitimate daughter of a well-known blue-blood. It was a terrible scandal during that time to have a child and be unmarried, so mother was certain that the child belonged to a high echelon's daughter. She was sure that this was the reason why the child had been stashed away with the village woman.

Although I'd thoroughly enjoyed this mystery story, disbelief always stayed close to the surface of my mind; that is, until many years later when it appeared again, but you're going to have to wait to hear about that disclosure.

CHAPTER 3

The Weekend Seminar

This time the door I was invited to open presented itself quite innocently. It was a secondhand bookstore that drew my attention. I entered the shop, not realizing that this decision would change my life forever. Being an avid reader, I'm always open to purchasing bargain books and on this particular day of idly browsing the shelves full of used paperbacks, found one that was written by a favorite actress. It was titled, *Out on a Limb*, by Shirley MacLaine. Heard of it? I bet you have! That dog-eared copy cost me a whole dollar, but its effect on my life has been priceless.

If you're old enough to remember, you may know of the tremendous amount of commotion this book caused after its release at the beginning of the 1980s. At that time, metaphysical thought was considered a New Age fad leftover from the hippy period of the 1960s. The general public considered it not to be taken seriously, just a bunch of whackos that were probably high on drugs. When *Out on a Limb* was published, negative and positive reactions came shooting out of the news media with the impact of thunderbolts. Many lives were changed because of McLain's disclosure of her extraordinary experiences, and her fame as an actress was almost overshadowed by the notoriety of her out-of-this-world revelations. She was a very gutsy lady to produce this book at that time, as the general public was still scoffing at the 1950s publication *The Search for Bridey Murphy*.

By this time, my reaction to reincarnation wasn't as negative as it had been during that Dream Workshop. After all, it had occurred some odd ten years previously, and although I still wasn't completely convinced that it was as factual as life itself, I was now open and eager to learn more. During the intervening years, I'd delved into literature on the subject and listened to more knowledgeable people than I talk on the subject. So, my mind was now ready for a deeper understanding of the concept.

But, believe it or not, I didn't purchase *Out on a Limb* because of its content. In fact, I had very little knowledge of the ruckus it had caused except for the publicity that latched on to it, and I tend to ignore sensationalism in the news media. On the contrary, my admiration of its author as an actress drew me to the book, and I was curious as to what she was writing about. It lay on my bedside table for a month, but when I finally decided to read it, I couldn't stop until I'd finished the last page. It gave me the strange sensation of already knowing what she was about to discuss before turning a page to read what she had to say. As I opened to the first page and started to read, a new doorway cracked open a little—but after finishing the whole thing, the entrance had been flung wide open and the invitation to go forward couldn't be ignored.

The book impacted my psyche so strongly that on an impulse I wrote to Shirley MacLaine and to my astonishment, got a reply. I've not forgotten one of the statements she made in that personal letter.

She stated, "We are living in such exciting times."

Exciting? Even in the 1980s, the world was having major problems, and as I read her letter and those lines, her thought processes puzzled me. They don't anymore. No one would deny that humanity's foundation is now in such a chaotic state that the present problems make the 1980s look like a minor earth tremor. So, I'll use the following analogy to illustrate what I believe she meant by using that word, "exciting."

Let's say you've decided to give your house a thorough spring-cleaning, and it's going to be the best cleaning it's ever had. You begin with the kitchen and decide to start with the cupboards. The first thing you have to do before you can clean the shelves is to empty them of their contents, right? Uggh! There's that outdated can of vegetables hiding at the back of a grubby shelf, and there's that bag of marshmallows you couldn't find when you needed them. They're probably as hard as a brick. After discarding food items that belong in the garbage, scrubbed the shelves of grime and sticky spills, cleaned the rest of the kitchen so that it looks spic and span, you go to your bedroom. You slide open the closet doors. Wow! That closet is a mess! You pull clothes from their hangers that are outdated or no longer fit. You pile them into boxes destined for Goodwill. And those scuffed shoes with the worn-down heels have definitely got to go. Windows are polished and spiders run for cover in fear of their lives.

Do you understand the analogy? Mother Nature's had enough of the built-up trash we've dumped onto this planet. She's cleaning up the mess we've made, and so volcanoes are erupting and earthquakes are making the land tremble. Oceans are polluted, and marine life is dying. The world is off its axis, and waters are rising as icebergs melt. Do you feel as I do that you're on the deck of a rolling ship that's in heavy seas and you're staggering like a drunken sailor? My friend, the world and its inhabitants are in the midst of a major "spring cleaning."

So is this condition exciting, as Shirley stated? Get out your dictionary and look up the word. It gives alternative words to describe its meaning: turbulent, frantic, stirring, tempestuous, and quaking. Shirley is right. We are living in exciting times, but that doesn't mean that we're enjoying the party. We are being given the opportunity to clean up our act before we move ourselves out of existence. But I'll get off my soapbox and return to my tale of the seminar.

A few months after receiving Shirley MacLaine's letter, I got another one, this time a generic missive. It was an invitation to attend a weekend seminar that she was planning to hold in a city close to where I live. She called it The Higher Self Seminar. I was working in a hospital and decided to take on extra shifts to earn money to pay for my attendance because although it wasn't too expensive, it was more than my usual budget allowed. One of my fellow nurses wanted to know why I was working such long hours, and I told her the truth.

She sarcastically responded, "Oh isn't she that actress who believes we're going to come back as a duck?"

As I've said already, some people have to return more than once to get it. But the reason for mentioning this incident is that it jogged a memory of a comment Shirley made concerning the value of money.

She opened her weekend workshop with the following statement. "I didn't want to charge too large an amount so that people who were meant to be here could afford it. At the same time, I didn't want to make it so inexpensive that some people would attend for all the wrong reasons."

I've never forgotten that piece of insightful wisdom, and in my work as a therapeutic, past life reader, have practiced the same sensitivity. I want people to come to me that need assistance and not have to worry about a large expense. On the other hand, I'm not a fortune-teller, so I don't want to make it too monetarily easy to see me, if this is what a person wants. Don't get me wrong, I'm not knocking fortune-telling. If having your future foretold makes you smile, that's fine. In fact, every once in awhile I also like to indulge myself in it, and along with a few friends I make a pot of tea and read their tea leaves. We all know, of course, that this is for entertainment only. Entering someone's past life can also be fun, but these insights always have a different purpose. They are directed by my Head Honchos toward guiding that person in certain areas of their life that need to be worked on.

To go into detail regarding the events of that weekend would take up too much of this communiqué. It's also unnecessary, as so much of the knowledge she covered relating to reincarnation was unknown during that time but has now spread much wider in the Western world, thanks to Shirley MacLaine as well as others of her ilk. More people in our Western culture are now open to its concepts and are giving it a voice. Suffice it to say that for me, the depth of knowledge and heightened awareness received from her seminar was akin to being launched in a rocket ship heading for Mars. My spiritual knowledge blasted forth and rose higher than I believed possible. The whole weekend was intensely personal for all the attendees, and like myself, I'm sure that each individual made a leap in their personal growth. I entered that weekend not knowing who I was and came away with the right answer. Her topic may have been reincarnation, but she went into minute detail as to the role of our existence; as to why each human is so important. Every piece of a jig-saw puzzle is needed in order to create the whole picture. If one person is missing, then the universal plan cannot be completed.

To say that Shirley MacLaine is an old soul is an understatement. I know that at least she impacted the lives of everyone at that seminar, not to mention the thousands of other lives that she's touched with her wisdom.

I'll also pass along another significant piece of advice she shared with the attendees, as it also applies to you- and you- and you. During that weekend, there was a session whereby she had volunteers walking among her audience with a microphone to answer any questions that they may have. One woman was so obviously overcome by this actress's fame that I'm still wondering if she retained anything of value from the seminar. The woman raised her hand so that a volunteer approached her and handed her the microphone. Instead of a query, this person began a breathless speech of adoration, voicing her complete reverence that this famous person had condescended to talk to mere mortals. She continued to repeatedly thank Shirley in a most gushing manner, until I felt embarrassment for the woman.

Shirley suddenly stopped her in mid-sentence and said, "I've got to give you a hug to let you know that I'm only human." With that, she left her place on the platform, approached the woman, and wrapped her arms around her body. After a minute or so, she returned to the podium and addressed every-one in a solemn tone. "Don't make me your guru," she said. "You are all your own gurus."

Amen! She's right on! I still feel a sense of power when remembering that statement.

When she made the comment in her book that "I am God," she was not being blasphemous as a lot of people thought. She was saying that we carry that divine spirit within ourselves and need to trust in that fact. After all, doesn't the Bible say that we are all made in His image? Honor yourself first, my friend, and everything else will fall into its rightful place.

The most profound truth gained from that weekend was that I knew exactly why I was here, and what I was meant to accomplish. The knowledge didn't manifest overnight, but that's where it started.

During that weekend with its intensive training, Shirley led a session whereby everyone was partnered with another person, and we focused on seeing a past life of our partner. We were at the end of our two-day seminar, and by this time, she had raised our consciousness to a much higher level. As I saw my partner's previous lives so easily and with such clear perspective, it felt as if this was not the first time I'd done this. It seemed to be a natural part of my psyche and this particular door seemed to open with a fanfare of rolling drums!

It would be a few years before I was asked to give readings in public venues, but the seeds that were unconsciously planted within me were nurtured that weekend. They eventually grew and manifested into the person I am today. Over these many years, I've found that in helping people on their life's journey, it's also helped me to understand my own life path. And, my sincere hope is that the other people at that workshop also found their own gifts and utilized them to help their fellow man. After all, at this significant time in our history, we all need as much help as we can get.

That weekend seminar showed me the contract I was meant to honor in this lifetime and it's made me grateful to know that this gift I've been given has helped hundreds of people who have sought answers to their own path in life. Let me say this friend, when an opportunity to use your own gift is presented to you, grab it with both hands and run with it!

I have to say though that the biggest gift that I've received is much more valuable, because in giving what I consider only ten percent of myself, I've received a hundredfold in return. Many strangers have trusted me with their personal lives, and by allowing me to enter their psyche, I've learned so much about the intricate nature that makes humanity tick. The spiritual expansion gained through my interactions with these people has no price ticket. You too will receive this same spiritual satisfaction if you share what you have with others.

As I write this, my wish is that you will also be given an opportunity to meet such a teacher, if you haven't already done so. I know that if you are ready to receive further wisdom, it will come to you, just as it did with me.

If I had not honed this gift, I would never have had the opportunity to meet so many people, and some have become dear friends. My gratitude to Shirley MacLaine is unending and yes, despite all the problems in our world, it's still exciting to be here. Of course, I'm now using that word "exciting" in its most positive connotation.

CHAPTER 4

The Crinoline Lady

The amount of insight I'd gained from the seminar had now left me with an unshakable belief in reincarnation. I didn't need any more validation, and so once again, my Head Honchos were about to show me another door that would allow me to continue the journey. Would I choose to go through it, or would I ignore it as I'd done when attending that dream group? What do you think? Although I'm not an expert swimmer, this time around I wasn't afraid to dive into the deep end of the pool. Even so, I didn't know that I would be plunging headfirst into depths I hadn't known existed. A whole new dimension was about to open up, and unreality became reality.

The latest key handed to me was a popular, live television show that was aired for the residents of the Pacific Northwest. It happened around the same time as the seminar had occurred, and people were staying home on Sunday nights to enjoy watching this popular program because of its unusual dynamics. The emcee would present two separate panels of guests to discuss the pros and cons of a current subject that was in the news headlines. This show's host knew how to activate controversy in the discussions, so that the opposing opinions among the participants made for some lively, sometimes heated conversations. If you lived in Oregon or southern Washington at that time, you may remember it as being called *Town Hall.*

The aftermath of Shirley MacLaine's book was still producing strong waves of opinion concerning reincarnation, and on one particular Sunday, the talk show centered on this subject. The participants were animated and argumentative, both for and against, and I sat glued to the television screen.

One of the guest speakers was a professional therapist with a string of impressive letters after her name. She was also a firm believer in reincarnation, and even more significant was the fact that she believed we carry physical as well as emotional problems into our present life that have manifested in a previous existence. In other words, that seemingly pure and unspoiled newborn is carrying unseen junk when it arrives here. Her former patients who suffered from physical ailments seemed to have been unresponsive to known medical healing. However, she claimed to have cured such patients by hypnotizing and guiding them through a former incarnation that had started the trauma. Once she learned what had originally caused the affliction, she could enact an appropriate cure. And to my ever present skeptical mind but nonetheless satisfaction, she had brought a former client with her who was to verify her claims.

This person sat next to her and had vigorously nodded his head in agreement as she had shared her beliefs with the studio audience and of course, the TV viewers. The therapist introduced him and he began to share his story. I could hardly wait to hear what he had to say. He was a burly man with a neck as thick as a bull that sat on broad shoulders. He had a rugged-looking face, and his overall persona would make a person think twice before challenging him to a fight. He began with a statement that he was employed as a long-distance truck driver. According to his tale, he had suffered from severe migraine headaches that were so incapacitating that they'd affected his ability to work. Unable to get relief from medications, he'd consulted this therapist. She'd hypnotized him into reliving a life in France during the French Revolution, where he had met his demise during this conflict by losing his head to the guillotine. I listened in fascination, absorbing all he had to say, and sardonically thought to myself, *that would give anyone a bad headache!* Needless to say, he claimed that he'd been cured of his migraines.

The following day, I called the TV station and learned that this therapist had an office in a nearby city. An idea had begun to germinate. I wanted this counselor to hypnotize me and see what would happen. As usual, and despite my fascination with this subject, I still questioned the validity of this counselor's claims. I needed personal proof because I couldn't quite wrap my head around the fact that the truck driver's words were the whole truth, and nothing but the truth. Oh ye of little faith!

And so, I decided that there's only one way to find out and called her office to make an appointment

• • • ● ● ● ● • •

Unsettling thoughts tumbled around inside my head like clothes being tossed in a dryer. My mind still vacillated between yes and no as I made my way up the steps to the door of the counselor's office. I'd never been hypnotized and doubted that I could be. *What am I getting myself into?* My Capricorn's task-master, Saturn, is always ready to surface with its dour outlook, and now its influence was working overtime on me. After all, wasn't I a strong-minded individual and always in control? *Could this well-respected professional really take me into a past life?* Even though I now believed in reincarnation, it was a whole different story when it came down to my own past history. *Did I really want to know who I had been in a previous lifetime? More importantly, even if she could hypnotize me, did I want to take the risk of being controlled by someone?* Ah! This latter thought caused an uncontrollable shudder to pass through my body. I'd never allowed anyone to control me—not even my parents. I shook my head to clear my brain of all the negativity, but the doubts wouldn't go away. *Oh well. For better or worse, here goes.* Shrugging my shoulders in an attempt to relieve the tension, I stood in front of the door—still hesitating. Taking a deep breath, I raised a hand and pressed the doorbell.

Never in my wildest dreams would I have imagined what was about to take place. I was completely unaware that this decision I'd made was about to impact my psyche and influence future decisions for the rest of my life . . .

The hypnotist's quiet voice started to lull me, and my body finally relaxed. As she began to talk me into a somnolent state, I became conscious only of her soft-spoken voice and the cushioned chair my body was reclining in. Then the room began to disappear . . . a sense of mysticism came over me; that feeling one gets just before falling asleep. Strange images were passing through my mind as if experiencing a precursor to a dream state. It felt as if I was a participant in one of those old TV dramas narrated by Rod Serling. Remember *The Twilight Zone*, with its strange images and catchy theme music?

Startling scenes began to flash in front of me as the voice continued to guide me down and down . . . deeper and deeper. Euphoria took over, and it was as if I was watching a movie, yet at the same time, I was the character in the story and not just sitting in the audience.

The hypnotic words grew fainter until it seemed as if they were only inside my head . . . My sub-conscious slowly opened to a past timeline . . .the voice seemed to be coming from a long way away, as if it were coming through an echo chamber . . .

It's the mid-1800s and I'm in a rural area of England. Taking a deep breath, I inhale the scents of springtime. Fruit trees are replete with pink and white blossoms that give the promise of bearing sweet, juicy crops. Newly born lambs gambol in meadows under the watchful eyes of placid sheep . . . I sense the sweet smell of new grass mixed with warm animal smells . . .once again, I inhale deeply and the spring air leaves a refreshing tingle on my tongue . . .

The outdoor scenery begins to fade. . . I'm in a house.

A girl of around five years of age is sitting on a fireside settle in the kitchen. A thick, hooked rug covers the stone-flagged floor, and a wooden table holds an unlit lamp in its center that leaves an oily scent in the air. Cooking utensils are scattered on the table, waiting to be used.

The child is writing on a slate with a piece of chalk that she holds in one of her chubby little hands. Her small feet rest on the stone fire-earth and the delicious odor of roasting meat is coming from a big, cast iron oven that's next to the burning fire.

It's her father's house, and the warm and cozy room is her favorite place to be. Thick, dark ringlets fall around her face as she leans forward in concentration, sticking out the tip of her tongue as she focuses on writing. She pauses in her endeavors to brush specks of chalk off her white apron that covers the blue muslin dress she's wearing.

The hypnotist's voice seems to be speaking to her from somewhere unseen.

"What is your name?"

Without any hesitation, the child starts to write the name "Elizabeth" on her slate.

"Where are your parents?" The voice asks.

She answers, "Papa is in his study, working on his papers."

"And your mother? Where is she?"

The child hesitates for a moment, wrinkling her brow in thought. "I'm not sure. Papa said she went to heaven. I don't remember her."

The voice continues to ask pertinent questions, such as her family name and the name of the place where she's living, to identify her surroundings and lifestyle. Without missing a beat, the girl answers in a child-like manner, even giving details that haven't been asked of her. She volunteers the information that she lives in Bagnall, adding, "It's a village."

Is this village near to a bigger town?"

"Not very near. Papa took me there once for an outing and it was such fun! It's called Nantwich."

She's a bright and friendly child.

Once the hypnotist is satisfied with the answers, she gently guides her subject forward.

"Move to a different time in your life; a time that is important to you."

It's Elizabeth's sixteenth birthday, and a celebration is taking place in the grand entrance hall. Candles light up the hall like a Christmas tree and the gaiety in the house is creating a glowing energy that is as bright as the flickering candles. Visiting guests mingle in groups, but most are vying for Elizabeth's attention. What a good time she's having! Her papa has given her an exquisite gold necklace encrusted with emeralds. It had belonged to her mama. The piece of jewelry encompasses her neck and complements her first grown-up evening gown. The gown is made of white satin, and its low scooped neckline sets off the necklace to perfection. Elizabeth fingers it as she chats with the people who have come to celebrate her birthday. She's feeling quite adult and is charming her guests with a self-confidence that belies her young years. Everyone remarks that she has the manner of a much older girl. *It's the happiest day of my life, and I love Papa so much! He is so good to me . . .*

"Can you move to another significant moment in your life?"

The mood has drastically changed. There's a pervading somberness in the air that covers everything in a heavy cloud . . .

The Manor House stands three stories high, including the attics. In a ground floor room Elizabeth is standing, peering out of a long, latticed window. Her dark eyes reveal her perplexed state of mind. *Where can he be?* Worrisome thoughts race through the young girl's head as she continues to stare at the empty, half-circular driveway outside the window. She moves the window's heavy drapes further to one side in the hope that this wider view will reveal him to be coming along the dirt lane that leads to the house. But the lane is empty. *Why doesn't he come as he promised?*

She remembers the many times when he'd visited and the thrill of hearing the trotting of his horse as the animal's hooves hit the graveled driveway leading to the entrance. It was always such an effort not to rush outside to greet him! Of course, proper young ladies must act with decorum when young men came courting.

It had taken many weeks for her father to accept his wooing, but miracle of miracles, her parent had finally stopped his objections! After all, wasn't her suitor descended from several generations of genteel folk? Their relationship really was socially suitable, and he'd eventually been grudgingly accepted as her lover's charm and impeccable manners finally won the protective parent's approval. Even though she was only seventeen—well, that is, almost—he was considered a quality suitor. Naturally, Meg always chaperoned them whenever they went for their rides together. Even so, the governess/companion was easily given the slip whenever they wanted to be alone, which was most of the time.

Again, her troubled mind returned to the present situation. *He's not coming.* The shocking truth finally hit home. Elizabeth's commonsense had to accept this fact. *If he were coming, he would have been here over an hour ago*

The last time they'd been together, she'd broken the news to him. She'd hesitated to tell him but had finally blurted it out. Of course, she'd expected him to be as shocked as she was, but it never entered her head that the pregnancy wouldn't lead to marriage between them. They loved each other so much! Elizabeth's thoughts had been centered on how her father would react to such news, rather than what her lover's response would be. Although his face had turned pale as she'd revealed her secret, he'd quickly regained his composure, and she'd felt so reassured when he'd declared his love and said that he would ask her father for her hand in marriage. Of course, she'd expected nothing less. Now, it started to dawn on Elizabeth that being with child had disturbed him more than she'd realized.

Meg moved closer to her side as if to protect her girl. She'd being taking care of Elizabeth for most of her life, and she was more like her own daughter. The woman was full of anxiety, knowing that she had to break the news to the child. How could she tell her that the local gossip told of his having departed the area? Some of the rumors even said that he'd left for the coast, planning to set sail for foreign parts.

Now Elizabeth would have to face her father alone . . .

Again, the voice came to her, guiding her to another event . . .

Thank God it's over! So much pain! She'd never have believed such intense pain existed. But now sweet heaven, her body could finally relax and she was oh, so eager to hold her daughter. Meg had told her the cries were that of a baby girl. *How proud he would have felt to see his child.* Elizabeth deliberately shut out the thought of him. Wherever he was, she had vowed never to think of him again. His betrayal was still as heart-wrenching as ever, but she now had a new life to live for, and the child was hers alone to cherish. *But where is she? Where is my baby? Why is my father looking so tight-lipped—and where is Meg?*

The parent stood at the end of the four poster bed, staring grim-faced at his disheveled daughter, her face wet with perspiration from the ordeal of labor. Her beautiful hair hung in limp, sweaty tendrils around her shoulders.

Elizabeth was exhausted and his words didn't register. *What is he saying? She's gone?*

"It's for your own good," her Papa was saying. "She'll be well taken care of, and you can carry on with your life as if this never happened."

All at once her foggy brain cleared. *No! He wouldn't take my baby away from me!*

The terrible wail was that of an animal caught in a trap. She needed to get away and realized that the agonizing scream was coming from deep inside her very soul. *Dear God! She had to get away from this nightmare! Gone! Her daughter had been taken away—such agony!*

"Move forward. NOW!"The command was urgent.

The voice was coming from someplace outside of herself. Just as she felt that her heart would break, a gossamer veil descended and the pain was blocked from her mind. Her hammering heart slowed down to normal and her breathing relaxed . . .

Elizabeth gave an audible sigh.

"Where are you now?"

She answered the voice that was coming from inside her head. "I'm taking care of my father's house."

The atmosphere in the home felt impoverished, its energy as malnourished as a pauper. It was as if its occupants were dead and the rooms their mausoleum.

Elizabeth stood in the doorway of Papa's study, observing the elderly man seated in his armchair in front of the fire hearth. He was staring with unfocused eyes into the flickering flames. Although the room wasn't cold, the glowing fire might as well have been dead ashes. The room was depleted of energy and felt as empty as the whisky glass on the table beside his chair . . .

"How old are you?"

Her brow wrinkled in thought, as if she'd lost all sense of time and age wasn't of any importance. "Maybe I'm in my late thirties, or thereabouts." She sounded listless.

Elizabeth felt so sorry for him. Seeing his still form as he leaned his stiffening body toward the warmth of the fire, she wished she could give him solace. She took note of the sad face and the deep shadows in eyes that had once sparkled with life. It seemed to have been forever since she'd seen him smile, and she knew that the apathy she saw wasn't from his advanced age. It went deeper than that. Without anything being said, Elizabeth knew her father regretted his actions all those years past that had deprived her of her child. Although he still hated her lover and angrily blamed him for ruining her life, she was well aware of the amount of guilt he suffered because of his own actions toward her.

Of course, she understood what had prompted him to act in such a cruel manner. Nevertheless, seeing his sadness as he sat with his thoughts, Elizabeth wanted to go to the man and comfort him; to explain that she had long since forgiven him. But this wasn't to be. The subject of the past remained unspoken, and life between the daughter and parent had taken on a daily routine of colorlessness, as if nothing had ever happened to shake the foundations of their world. A silent acceptance of their lot had been created that only grew deeper as the years passed. From her stance in the doorway, Elizabeth observed her father's bent frame, realizing that she couldn't breach the gulf that lay between them.

The woman was only too aware of that tragic time in her life. The memory never left her, even though she unquestionably understood her father's position. Should it have been revealed that she had a child out of wedlock, her scandalous behavior would have ruined them in the eyes of their friends and society. Even the village people would have looked askance at them, although propriety would have forbidden their voicing any opinions. Yes, Elizabeth couldn't fault her father for his actions, but it had created this deep divide between them.

Outsiders looked on the pair as perfect examples of devotion. They thought she'd never married because of her loyalty to him and the need to fill the duties that his late wife would otherwise have accomplished. It was as it should be.

The woman with the prematurely graying hair continued to stand in the doorway, watching the old man with sadness in her heart. She'd long since become resigned to her fruitless life. It was inevitable. The times they lived in didn't allow for improprieties, especially such shocking behavior as producing a bastard child. Again, Elizabeth sighed in resignation and walked away from the studio door - disappearing into the mists of time . . .

"What is happening now?"

The years had gone by. The woman was in her boudoir, lying on her four-poster bed. A heavy down quilt was tucked around her chin and only thin, white arms were exposed on top of the comforter. Long, straggly hair hung about the elderly person's head. The unkempt strands were as white and as fine as goose down. No longer was there a hint of the thick black curls that young Elizabeth had once proudly worn. The transparent face lay in repose with purple-tinged eyelids closed as if in sleep. But she wasn't sleeping. Elizabeth was dying. The only light in the room came from candles sitting on mahogany tables at either side of the bed and a fire that burned brightly in the bedroom's brick fireplace. Elizabeth was alone. It was what she wanted. After all, hadn't she been alone for most of her life? The intermittent exhalations of breath gradually became slower and slower. With each passing moment, the length of time between them became longer. Suddenly, Elizabeth gave a rasping sigh. She was gone.

• • • ● ● • •

Aftermath

It took days for me to come down to earth after experiencing this drama, and my mind was in a state of limbo. It was as if the mind straddled a fence between this world and that of the Victorian existence. A major block in my psyche had been penetrated and my sub-conscious was no longer hidden. Recalling this previous life had proved without doubt that life didn't end with the death of a body, and I'd made a significant leap. Life no longer had boundaries.

As always, it had been my choice to go through that particular door and despite having this lingering sense of unreality, the event seemed to be such a logical conclusion to certain events in my present life. The conviction that this life I was now living was preplanned had been confirmed, and I felt a sense of completion in more ways than one. Let me explain, friend, because my experience is not unique. As I've already conveyed to you, the life you are now living is only a few pages of a story that has not yet concluded.

I'll start by trying to give you an understanding of all the intricacies of Universal Law; that is, the full meaning of Cause and Effect. By dissecting this past life experience in relationship to my present existence, the intention is to give you a deeper understanding of your own life. It will help you to gain a sharper knowledge of all the reasons why you are traveling your personal path and will provide a better perspective as to certain conditions in your life. It will enlighten you as to why you have certain personality traits: likes and dislikes actions and reactions. Maybe it will give you a better understanding as to why you gravitate to certain relationships and your reactions toward people you meet. Even your choice of profession may come into play. If your personality is completely unlike your parents or siblings and you're wondering why this is so, consider the fact that it's because you've brought back your unique self from a previous incarnation. So here goes.

First of all, you return with the same entities that have been with you in other lives. These are the main characters in your life's play and have the biggest influence on you. I call these people your cluster group. Think of your life as a stage play with the main actor/actress (you) as its starring player. Those folks playing supporting roles are your personal cluster group. That isn't to say that we don't meet other people in life that we may not have met before, but I call these latter encounters ships that pass in the night, or bit-players. In any event, your cluster group is the most important element in your life.

Usually this group consists of your parents, siblings, relatives, spouses . . . I'm sure you get the picture. This is followed by less important players who come and go throughout your life, such as co-workers, bosses, childhood friends—even that teacher that influenced your life either in a positive or negative way. Secondly, when we return following a former lifetime, we sometimes swap roles with another significant (cluster) person. This usually happens when a role reversal might be necessary for our spiritual development. I'll use a simple example of such a situation: a rich man in his mansion without a care in the world may have to return and experience the problems of being poor and/or homeless in another life.

The following dissection of my former life as Elizabeth will show you such reversals and how my cluster group was now reacting to these reversals due to past experiences. Remember, my life is not dissimilar to yours, my friend. It also can, and does happen to everyone—even you. Cause and effect is as inevitable as night following day. Before you've come to the end of this book, you may come to the realization that someone in your own life is in a role reversal. It may even be you.

So, what had Elizabeth's life taught me? And, after I'd found the answer to this question, how was I to handle the mistakes from that life? What could I do to improve my spiritual self this time around? Ah! Yes, this latter question really is the number one reason why we all incarnate. As I found myself asking this one question, I began to dissect that other life.

The most obvious answer I'd received was to the number one puzzle in my present life. It had shown me who the unknown person was in my father's maternal ancestry. Remember the story of the illegitimate child who had been my great-grandmother? She was the daughter of Elizabeth, of course! This mystery had easily been resolved.

Of course, unbeknownst to me, I was given a clue to this during the 1970s when I shared my past life dream at that workshop. I had been given a flashback to myself as Elizabeth. The memory of the attitude I'd displayed at that meeting still makes me blush with embarrassment, but luckily, my Head Honchos are very patient as they had waited until I was ready to digest this information before they showed me that door again. Now that the illegitimate child's parentage had been revealed, it made perfect sense. After having re-experienced this former life, I was now being given a chance to finish this particular chapter. It was no longer a case of walking blindly through a dark tunnel. The tunnel was now well lit, and the present took on more significance.

Over the years, I've come to think of that Victorian life as my wasted life. At the first challenge I'd been presented with, I'd folded and run like that cowardly lion from The Wizard of Oz. And, as a daughter of a controlling father and living in a moralistic society, I had succumbed to a dual pressure: a controlling father and the narrow-minded society that existed during that time period. Even so, this was no excuse for having abandoned my responsibilities. Regardless of the puritanical lifetime I had lived in, I should have owned my child and not been subservient to that which my father and society expected of me. As it was, the rest of my life had been spent hiding from myself. Fear, my friend, is our biggest bugaboo. Don't allow fear to rule your life. One might make the excuse that the attitudes of that Victorian era had dictated my choices in life. Not a good excuse. If you learn nothing else in your life but this one thing, be true to yourself. "Unto thine own self be true."

As I now look back on my present life, I can honestly say that I've lived it to its fullest. I've never hesitated to face life's challenges and deal with them. Unlike my life as Elizabeth, I don't run away from problems. However, balance in one's life is a necessity, and I now realize that I haven't always chosen to be balanced. In retrospect, as I look back on my childhood and occasionally my adulthood, I know that I've sometimes gone overboard with the independent attitude.

Beware of going to the opposite extreme in your actions. The effect is that of trying to balance a see-saw that you're riding. When there is too much weight on one end and not enough on the other, it's hard to control the ride. One rider is going to be hanging helplessly in the air while the other is sitting on the ground, unable to rise. I realize that my life now, when comparing it to the life during that nineteenth century, has at times gone from the sublime to the ridiculous. Being a non-confrontational pushover (Elizabeth) is not good, but neither is being a stubborn mule! Like I've said, you bring back personality traits from previous lives, and when it's a reversal of a role you have played, you have to make sure that you don't overact and give a ham performance. Always be aware that in any of your actions, balance is the key word. Keep that see-saw ride stable.

Let me recap. Before you were born, you made a contract to work on certain issues so that consciously or sub- consciously, you are working on these commitments. So live your life mindfully by honoring your existence. Know this my fellow traveler—your life may have its warts, and you may think that it's not always fair, but overall you are so lucky to have the opportunities that being human provides. The biggest opportunity that you have as a human is to honor your spiritual self by appreciating the gift of Life.

Now, let's return to the business of dissecting that Victorian life. The most amazing occurrence I'll share with you while under hypnosis is that not only did I know I was Elizabeth, but I was also aware that the people who were with me in that former existence, had returned to influence my present life. Let me be clear about this because your life follows the same basic pattern with your personal cluster group. Their clothes and mannerisms may have changed, but they are still the same spiritual entities that you've encountered on life's stage before this lifetime.

I'd returned with my cluster of people but they were now playing reverse roles.

Let's start with the faithless lover in that life. He had now reentered the stage to play the role of my second husband.

Several years after divorcing my children's father, I remarried. Not only was Don a kind and loving man to me, but also a good father to the children from that former marriage. His quiet strength and loyalty made me feel as if I'd landed at an oasis after that turbulent first marriage. My only complaint was that he was so overly protective toward me that at times I felt suffocated. At such times I would irritably accuse him of wanting my attention twenty-four by seven! He acted as if he was afraid to let me out of his sight.

Aha!! The light switch had turned on. That playground ride was now almost topsy-turvy!

I bet you've already got the picture. Yes, he'd played the role of the faithless lover and left me alone to face the consequences of our actions. In his coward-ice, he'd flown the coop. So, what was happening now? He was now reversing his role, of course. He was taking care of me to the point of suffocation! He was <u>overcompensating.</u> In Don's eagerness to right the wrong he'd inflicted in that Victorian relationship, he was now going too far overboard in making sure that he protected me. He'd returned with a load of guilt from that former life, and in his sub-conscious mind, the betrayal he'd shown toward me had to be rectified. But he was straddling that see-saw up in the air, unable to come down because a three-hundred-pound giant (guilt) was sitting on the ground at the other end! See what I mean by role reversal?

And what was my part in all this? Knowing whence his fear of losing me came from, I changed my reactions to his overly protective manner. Instead of becoming irritated with him, I would thank him for being so caring and reassure him that he wasn't going to lose me. It worked.

But who was the person who had played the part of my father? Answer? He was now my youngest child, reversing the role from dominating parent to not-so-perfect child ,(Elizabeth). He was the only boy in the family with three older, doting sisters,

46

Danny was a precocious kid with no fear of danger and skillful at getting what he wanted, especially from his sisters and mother. His teenage years were especially challenging, as he spent as much time as he could in seeking out trouble, and I have to say that I came by my gray hair honestly. To say that he was irresponsible is an understatement. Added to this problem was the traumatic relationship (or nonexistent relationship) between him and his step-father. They clashed constantly, and the toxic jealousy between them was a ticking time bomb. By returning with all the hate and guilt they both carried toward each other from that former life, they were now overreacting. Stability was definitely needed. Didn't I tell you that the universe doesn't miss a trick? But that wasn't the end of all that universal psychology.

As a moralistic parent in that Victorian lifetime, Danny was now hell-bent on not being so straight-laced once again. Did he now have to experience the irresponsibility that my lover had displayed? Was he going to extremes in making mistakes because he had to experience the mistake that Elizabeth had made? Mmmm ... as the saying goes, "What goes around comes around." Danny's animosity toward Don and my husband's toward my son had carried over into their present lives. The antagonism between them had been reignited, and this reversal of roles was a major bomb fire! What a mess!

So what do you think I should do to correct their problem?

Not a thing.

In that lifetime as Elizabeth, I'd been shown all too painfully that attempting to control another person's willpower causes irretrievable damage. And so, instead of worrying about their loud and regular clashes and my useless efforts to intervene, I opted to stop allowing them to push my buttons. Instead of trying to be the peacemaker, I distanced myself—physically and mentally. Each time a clash happened between them, instead of attempting to come between them to solve their animosity, I'd leave the house. I knew I had to let them figure out their karmic lesson for themselves. I couldn't control their free will. And, even more significantly, I would no longer allow them to control mine.

So, fast forward. Danny is now a father, and I sometimes chuckle to myself when I see him with his children. He's strict but fair. They love him, and he's a good father. But even though they know that when he says no he means it, he doesn't try to control their will.

Don passed away before I was ready to let him go, but he'd accomplished what he'd come here to do. Yet, he's still around and still watching over me. Luckily, he and my son made their peace before he left, and so maybe, just maybe, they won't have to return to do it all over again. At least, for their sakes, I hope not!

Oh, let me not forget Meg, the loyal governess and companion. She returned in this life as my older sister who had to do a lot of babysitting of me, and I suspect there were many times when she resented this responsibility. Regardless, we had chosen to return as sisters rather than non-relatives as the prior bond was still there.

And what of Elizabeth's lost child? She returned as my beloved, oldest daughter, and I learned, albeit painfully but consolingly, that there is no finality in death—only another chapter in the continuing story.

And so, dear reader, that former life that has impacted my present life's experiences is just an example of the many intricacies of reincarnation. There is so much more to paying karmic debts than we realize. All of life's events and actions are more purposeful than we can imagine. I will say it again because it's so important to understand. If you goof up in one life, you are given another chance to correct your mistakes in the present. You don't always have to wait to come back to correct them. You always have the opportunity to learn and grow from past mistakes in your present existence; more than once if necessary. All you have to do is to remember that balance is the key word. The goal is always to work toward perfecting the spiritual self so we can return to the Light that is Home.

In life, there is no such thing as good or bad, only experiences. And whatever injury we've inflicted on another, we have to remember that we are inflicting on ourselves. If we are a powerful tycoon and disregard those workers who have helped us to achieve that power, we may have to return and experience the struggles and pains of a worker. We are hurting ourselves when we harm another because there is no separation, except on this earth plane.

• • • • • • • •

Knowing that I demand lots of validation, my ever-patient guides have given me plenty of this regarding Elizabeth. Shortly after this event with the hypnotist had taken place and because I felt more grounded (ah), I decided I'd do some investigating into Elizabeth's family name. As indicated to me while under hypnosis, her family was well-known in the particular area of England where she had lived. And so, I thought *it shouldn't be too hard to locate her family tree if I do some serious digging.* By the way, don't hesitate to seek validation for yourself whenever you need it. You'll find that your guides will be more than willing to assist you.

They certainly made it easy for me because in a city near to my home, a Mormon library held hundreds of books, photos, and documents—all the paraphernalia that anyone needs to trace their ancestry. Of course, we now have sophisticated Internet companies that will help you to search for your ancestors but this was unheard of in the 1980s, so thank goodness this church is so thorough in documenting such information.

This Mormon Library is a large building and very organized. After telling the woman at the information desk what I needed, she directed me to a well-stacked section of a room that contained several shelves full of books dealing with English family heritages. In less than an hour, I had found what I needed. Bagnall and the county in which it was located was listed in a small non-descript book that specifically dealt with English counties and their villages. Great! I scanned the pages, and my eyes eventually locked on an item that mentioned Bagnall's local church. To my utter astonishment, but nonetheless satisfaction, I read that a minister of this church bore Elizabeth's family name. What more validation did I need?

Believe it or not, I felt a need for more proof. Let's just say that British people don't have a bulldog reputation for nothing. I was left wondering what else I could do to gain more facts that would convince me of having existed in this former lifetime.

The opportunity arose a short time later when my husband and I decided to take a trip back to visit my relatives in England and I planned to seek out that house in Bagnall, if it really existed. Remembering that under hypnosis I'd revealed that I lived near to a town called Nantwich, we planned on exploring this town and from there, make enquiries as to Bagnall's location.

After our arrival in England and as soon as possible we drove to this well-known place, which happens to be a quaint old-time market town. It was less than a couple of hours' drive from where I was born, so we had no trouble finding it. The day we visited happened to be the day of the weekly farmer's market, and the streets were crowded with shoppers meandering through the merchant's stalls. By the glances that came our way as we mingled with the crowd, I suspect peoples' curiosity was aroused when they heard my husband's American accent. Using this to our advantage, we asked a couple of people if they knew where a place called Bagnall was, but nobody seemed to have heard of it. Finally, I hit on the idea of going to the office of the town's church to make inquiries. England's rural townships always have a parish church that usually dates back hundreds of years to when its leaders ran the operations of the town. These churches always keep detailed records of the parish history, and this particular town has a beautiful, ancient church that dominates a spot in the town center.

We climbed the church steps and entered the foyer. Immediately I noticed a sharp contrast in its atmosphere, compared to the noisy and bustling marketplace. The sudden silence and solitude was comforting. A highly polished table made of a dark wood, sat to the left of the foyer and held the usual church pamphlets and a prayer box. The smell of beeswax mingled with a faint tangy odor of dead flowers. The flag-stoned floor looked cold, but the foyer was warm as heat came from an old-fashioned radiator that sat against one wall. We noticed a heavy wooden door that was darkened with age, was situated in the right wall of the foyer. It held a sign that read "Office," so we approached it and pushed down on its old fashioned iron latch. The door swung open with ease and we stood hesitating at the threshold of a room.

A middle-aged woman sat behind a fairly new looking oak-wood desk. Glancing around the room I noticed that it had been modernized and plenty of light came through a window that looked as if it had been widened from its original, old-world design. Standard metal files were arranged around the room. The only decorations were a large, ornate crucifix hanging on one wall and a framed map of the town and surrounding areas on an opposite wall.

The woman was busy typing, but as we stood hesitating, she lifted her head and asked, "Can I help you?"

Her enquiring voice sounded efficient as if she were used to answering visitors' questions, but this was the wrong time of the year for tour groups and her face held the same curious expression as those displayed by the shoppers in the market place. We were strangers to the town, but regardless, did we really look like tourists?

Her light-brown hair showed strands of gray and was pulled back to form an attractive bun at the nape of her neck. She was sitting and eying us with frank curiosity from over the top of rimless glasses. The woman reminded me of an older version of the comedian and actress Eve Arden, but her demeanor certainly wasn't reminiscent of the character played by Miss Arden. This person didn't appear to be the kind that wasted her time on frivolity. She was polite, but it was obvious from her body language and the papers that scattered her desk top that we were disturbing her in the middle of work.

Don spoke, "Excuse us for disturbing you, but we are wondering if you know where the village of Bagnall is?"

A look of surprise came over the woman's face at the sound of my husband's American accent, and I guessed at her thoughts: *What are Americans doing here when it isn't the tourist season?*

She quickly recovered her equilibrium and answered, "Why, yes. Bagnall is about three miles south of town, but it's nothing but a community of farmers."

The curiosity in her voice told me that she was wondering why Americans wanted to see a place that was most probably a speck on a map. Shouldn't we be in London visiting the usual tourist sites?

I quickly thought up an excuse. "I grew up in England, and many years ago, a relative of mine lived in Bagnall, so we thought we'd like to see the place." I wasn't actually lying, was I?

Apparently my English sounding accent and the plausible answer seemed to satisfy her because she visibly relaxed and—she almost smiled! Giving us explicit driving directions to Bagnall, she even expressed her hope that we'd have a good visit.

Don laughed as we hurried down the church steps. "Maybe she thought the Yanks were invading!"

As we drove out of town and picked up the main road she'd indicated, a smattering of raindrops began to fall. Weather in England is unpredictable in early spring, and it had been raining on-and-off all day. The church secretary had said three miles, but we seemed to have driven further, and I hoped we hadn't missed the lane that led to the hamlet.

"Slow down! I think that's the signpost." I pointed excitedly to a small sign that was a few yards ahead. It had started to rain in earnest and the road became barely visible through the spattered windshield.

As Don activated the windshield wipers and drove the car closer to the signpost, we saw that it stood at an entrance to a narrow lane. It wasn't very visible from the main road, being almost hidden by tree limbs, but sure enough, it showed the name Bagnall with an arrow pointing the way. Don turned into the entrance, and immediately we were driving over a dirt road that was full of rutted, rain-filled potholes. It was so narrow that should another car have been coming toward us, we'd have had a hard time squeezing past each other. As Don gingerly steered the car around the potholes, the rain suddenly stopped. *At least that's a blessing!* I thought. Even so, the dark clouds still looked ominous. We slowly cruised along, occasionally passing cottages, but the only signs of human habitation were lights that peeked through the homes' curtained windows. It seemed like the lane stretched forever, but after a couple of miles it came to a dead end, and we had to stop. I couldn't believe what I was seeing at the end of the lane.

---- *No way!* My eyes almost bugged out of my head as I sat staring through the windshield at an image in front of me. I was looking at a three-storied, redbrick house that was built in the Georgian style of architecture. It stood blocking any further progress.

I was in a state of shock.

My addled brain took in the front façade that showed several long, latticed windows that went almost to the ground and rose halfway up the side of the house. They ended just below their second-story counterparts. What appeared to be small attic windows below the roof were set in overhanging eaves. The ground level windows were bare of curtains or shades, and I could see cardboard boxes inside, piled against them. The place looked lonely and empty of people.

I broke out in goose bumps as I sat taking in this house with its half-circled, gravel driveway, and an involuntary shiver passed through my body. I felt as if someone had walked over my grave. This was Elizabeth's home. While under hypnosis, I had seen myself standing at one of those lower, latticed windows as I'd waited for my lover to appear. The only difference between the two views was that I had been inside the house, not outside. I'd seen that graveled driveway that ended in a half circle from a different angle. This was not déjà-vu or imagination, or even hypnosis. This was stark reality.

I turned my head to look at Don. He sat in silence. Not saying a word, I opened the car's passenger door and got out. Standing in the lane, I attempted to absorb with my eyes what my brain was telling me. It definitely was not my imagination or a dream. Being the ever-skeptical individual that I am, I know that deep down, I'd really questioned the story I'd experienced in that hypnotist's room with its scenes of this very same house. I'd occasionally wondered if the whole scenario I'd experienced while under hypnosis was just my impressionable mind working overtime. I could no longer have any doubts.

"Shall we take a look around the church?"

In my stupor, I hadn't noticed that Don had joined me. I also hadn't been aware of the small gray-stoned church a few yards to the right of the house. I'd been so stunned by actually seeing this former home that my focus had been on nothing else. We slowly approached the church and saw that it sat in the middle of a graveyard surrounded by an iron fence. The whole place looked as neglected as the house.

"Do you think Elizabeth's grave might be in there?" Don was voicing the same thought that was going through my mind.

Don pushed on the gate and it groaned and moaned in protest, but after he lifted it slightly, it swung open. Nobody had bothered to lock it. Our feet squished through mud as we made our way along the dirt path leading to the church entrance. I was hoping that inside we might find church records telling of Elizabeth's family. Climbing the worn steps to the entrance, I tried turning the big steel ring hanging from the heavy-looking door, but unlike the gate it was locked. Once more I tried it, but it was firmly bolted. The door wouldn't budge, and I felt let down. *What now?*

"Let's look around the graveyard," Don suggested.

Why not? Maybe we can still find her grave, I thought. My feet were cold as I tramped through the wet grass in between the gravestones. They were very old, and some lay flat in the ground among dandelion weeds. Most of the carvings on the grave stone markers were unreadable, and those that were visible, dated as far back as the seventeenth century. But we didn't find a marker bearing Elizabeth's name. The entire place reeked of damp earth mixed in with the bitter smells of weeds and crabgrass. The end of March was not a good month in England, weather-wise, and my exposed hands and face felt like ice. It seemed as if I were being touched by phantoms.

The threatening black clouds suddenly burst and rain began to pour in earnest. Although we both wore rain gear, we were quickly becoming soaked.

"This is silly," Don said. "We're never going to find anything in this downpour. Let's go!"

Making a dash for the car, Don turned on the ignition and punched in the heater to warm the interior as we shook ourselves like wet dogs. *Maybe we aren't meant to find her grave. Maybe seeing her home is all I needed.* Once more, I sat staring at the house, and it was as if my guides were chastising me. "Enough is enough! We've shown you where you lived. What more proof do you need?"

* * • • ⬤ ⬤ • • *

Assimilating all this was a major task unto itself, but I was certain of one thing: I would never have anymore doubt that our lives are already planned before we are born. I know that even though we have a free will to make our own choices, we can never deviate from the original plan, even if we choose a longer route to get there. Sometimes we are even smart enough to follow the right road to our destination!

We may choose a dead-end road (no pun intended) and have to turn around to start all over again, or we might skip the joy of viewing the scenery as we speed along the highway at eighty miles an hour, but we will still wind up where we are supposed to be. That is a fact.

We are always given another opportunity to get things right. Instead of calling it karma or pay-back time or cause and effect, the Bible prefers to call it reaping what you sow. Some of us are pretty stubborn, and we keep returning like a boomerang, continuing to sow weeds until we learn to plant a productive crop. All this happened many years past, but the memory will stay with me as solid as that Georgian brick house.

CHAPTER 5
A Psychic Television Encounter

The Lady of The Medieval Court

During the end of the 1980s my husband and I produced a quarterly newsletter that featured reviews of the latest metaphysical books and any item of a metaphysical nature. We named it *Friends Review*, and what started merely as a fun hobby quickly became very popular among readers, not to mention the publishers of such material. We would review the latest books, videos, and objects such as tarot cards that would coincide with their distribution to bookstores. It was then shipped to bookstores to be given to their customers as a freebie. Within one year, it had snowballed into being read in all fifty states and also a few other countries via subscriptions. Publishers advertised with us as it boosted their sales, and although we never made a profit from it, payments received from advertising kept it afloat. Not only did it provide us with excellent reading material, but it also introduced us to hundreds of like-minded people, and we both thoroughly enjoyed producing it. Sadly it was discontinued in 1994 following my husband's demise as I didn't have the expertise or the desire to operate it alone.

It was during the time of its popularity that I received a phone call from a person who introduced herself as Reverend Donna. She said that she was the minister of a non-denominational church located in a Washington city. She also explained that she had a weekly TV talk show that was broadcast around the Pacific Northwest and this was the reason for her call. She explained that her program was a live talk show that was geared toward psychic phenomena. The format was always a discussion with a guest speaker that would cover a variety of paranormal activities. Of course it drew the attention of viewers with metaphysical mindsets, and she asked if I would be interested in being a guest on her program and talk about *Friends Review*. Would I! What an opportunity to advertise our publication. We set a date for my appearance, and she gave me driving directions to the TV station. The state of Washington is just a few miles across the Columbia River from Portland, Oregon and the location of the TV station is in the city of Vancouver (not the one in Canada.) This Vancouver sits on the Washington side of the Columbia River and it would take roughly an hour to drive there from my Oregon home.

On the given day, I arrived early so that Reverend Donna and I could get to know each other. We chatted backstage for a while, and when the conversation came around to reincarnation, she let me know that she'd heard that I was a psychic and could tap into past lives. Trying to ignore the usual disquiet at the title that had been laid on me, I did confirm that my ability to see past lives was indeed true.

By this time, I was well into giving past life readings at metaphysical events and also had clients that visited my home for private readings. Added to this, I gave public talks on reincarnation at various venues in Oregon and other western states. In a nutshell, I'd got my feet wet.

It was almost time for the cameras to roll, so the reverend walked me to the studio's stage and indicated that I should sit next to her in our camera positions. The studio seated roughly fifty people in the audience section and it was full. *Obviously, her show is popular,* I thought as I scanned the rows of seated people. The lights dimmed, and the audience became barely visible as spotlights hit the stage. I blinked my eyes to adjust to the sudden brilliance as they focused on the reverend and me.

Reverend Donna asked good questions about *Friends Review*, and I answered appropriately. Feeling relaxed and enjoying this new experience, I felt positive energy radiating from the silent audience. It felt good.

Somehow she managed to switch the conversation to the subject of reincarnation, and before I realized it, she'd started to discuss my abilities to see past lives. She had changed the subject so smoothly, it was barely noticeable. Even so this switch didn't faze me, until she hit me with an unexpected request that literally knocked my socks off!

"Would you mind giving a reading for someone in the audience?" she asked.

Excuse me? At this point, I'd never given a reading within such a public forum as this, although in later years, I was to make several appearances on TV talk shows under similar circumstances. But this was early days of using the gift I'd been handed, and I hadn't yet learned of the unlimited power that the universe can deliver. You see, up to this point I'd had no reason to test the limits of the sub-conscious psyche. What was I to do now? *If I refuse, the audience and folks watching TV at home are going to think I'm a quack,* I thought. *On the other hand, if I agree to do this and can't perform in such a public environment, I will still be in trouble.* Reverend Donna had suddenly placed me in a heck of a pickle!

Then, a light switch turned on inside my head, and a mental voice said, *have faith, Marie.* It suddenly dawned on my slow-thinking brain that my Head Honchos would never lead me into a situation that I couldn't handle. In fact, when it came to working with spirit, they bent over backward to help when needed. This time I definitely needed supernatural help but instinctively knew they wouldn't let me down.

As I nodded my head in consent, the reverend addressed the audience. "Anyone who would like a past life reading, please raise your hand."

Many people lifted their hands in response, and my eyes swept over the rows of seats. Even though the peoples' images were dim beyond the stage lights, a woman in the second row caught my eye and I randomly selected her.

Trusting that my guides were steering me right, I closed my eyes, dismissed the studio and its attendees, and prepared to enter into an alternate state.

As I moved into my special, sub-conscious place, the studio surroundings began to fade. Eventually the room full of people disappeared and I was suspended in timelessness . . .

My body gave an involuntary shiver as I felt cold, damp air surround me. My sense of smell picked up a strange mixture of the scents of cloves, sage, and perfumed sashays that reminded me of pomanders worn by people of centuries past to mask the odor of unwashed bodies . . .

The present had vanished . . . I was in a different time and place . . .

A scene began to form in my inner vision and gradually became clearer. A medieval castle appeared . . . I was someplace in England . . . maybe its capital of London . . .

My sub-conscious guided me into a large and well-furnished room in the castle, but although fine woven tapestries hung on the walls to keep out the drafts, the room still felt cold and I mentally wrapped my arms around my chilled body . . .

A woman stood in the middle of the room. She was beautiful. Standing tall and proud, she seemed to be a woman of distinction, and the phrase, "This is a Lady of the Court" entered my head. Her attire was in the elaborate and confining style of the sixteenth century. She wore a gown of a wine-colored hue with long, flowing sleeves and the low neckline showed lots of elaborate, white lace trimming. Strands of creamy pearls and bright diamonds hung around her long, graceful neck. The bodice of the dress was tightly bound and exposed a delicately curving bosom above the low neckline, while an extremely full skirt made wide by layers of skirts underneath it swept the stone-flagged floor. Tendrils of light-colored hair peeped out from a tight fitting cap that resembled a nun's wimple. Still, the physical beauty of this woman could not compete with the radiant personality that shone through. She seemed to light up the room with a much brighter glow than the flames of a fire that burned in a huge stone earth. Many candles also cast their light around the room. I felt a sense of light-hearted exuberance and impulsiveness emanating from her; as if this lady enjoyed challenging life . . .

The knowledge came to me that this medieval woman was now sitting in the second row of the studio audience during our present timeline.

King Edward VI was on England's throne, having taken over from his father, the despotic King Henry V111.

Let me digress for a moment, dear reader. In the event that you don't know anything about this part of English history, I'll give you a brief introduction. Although King Henry had six wives, he only had one surviving son, Edward. He did have two daughters that were older than Edward, namely the princesses Mary and Elizabeth, later to become England's reigning monarchs. Queen Mary was the daughter of his first wife and came to the throne after the death of Edward. After her death, she was followed by the first Queen Elizabeth, who was the daughter of his second wife, the infamous Anne Boleyn. Although Edward was the son of Henry's third wife (Jane Seymour), it was always the male heir who inherited the throne, no matter how young he was or how many older sisters he had. A female would take over only if there were no male heir. Edward didn't reign very long as he died in his late teens, hence his sisters were then allowed to rule. No Women's Liberation Movement in those days and Henry would no doubt have chopped your head off if you had suggested such a thing as women's rights! Edward was only twelve years old when he became king, which led to having elected regents basically running the country; that is until the young king reached an age when he could rule without them. Inevitably, this situation caused much vying for political power over Edward and the chopping off of heads didn't end with Henry V111. As you are no doubt already aware of, insatiable political greed and fighting for power is not something our present century invented.

And so, let's get back to our medieval lady.

As my sub-conscious sojourned through this past era, I saw that this lady's influential position in Kind Edward's court allowed her to play political games that she thoroughly enjoyed. Knowing this, politicians took advantage and used her for their own agendas. Her impulsive nature thought it to be daring and exciting to be a go-between for the various political factions who were scheming for favorable advantages with Edward. Passing highly secret political information between the court's powerful regents was a great game as far as she was concerned, and it never entered this foolish woman's head that the game was dangerous. She was walking on thin ice . . .

The scene changed, and I saw the back of this Lady of the Court as she walked along a wide corridor of the castle. The end of the corridor was shrouded in an ominous black mist, and I felt a sense of foreboding. She was in trouble . . .

The vision faded and my subconscious became a blank . . .

Slowly returning from this other century, my eyes watered as the harsh glare of the TV lights once again hit me. I was back in the studio, sitting on the stage with the silent audience staring up at me. As I adjusted to my surroundings on the stage, I leaned toward the woman in the second row to see her more plainly through the lights, and asked her if the scenario I'd relayed made any sense to her. She nodded her head vigorously and mouthed the words "thank you."

The show ended and there was enthusiastic applause from the audience. The response seemed to have also pleased Reverend Donna as she said, "After the show, the staff and I always meet for lunch at a restaurant not too far from here. Would you like to join us?"

Accepting her friendly offer, I followed her out of the building.

The restaurant was within walking distance of the studio and on entering, the hostess led us to a long table with a "Reserved" sign on its pristine white tablecloth. Obviously the TV folks had a standard weekly reservation. It was the only large table in the room and was set with water glasses and cutlery for several people. Three of the TV crew-members were already seated, and Reverend Donna made the introductions as we seated ourselves.

I gave a casual glance around the room as we waited to be served and noticed that the rest of the room had smaller tables strategically placed, but only a few were occupied. My idle perusal landed on a table by a window a few yards away and to my surprise, there sat the woman who had been the recipient of my reading. She was alone. A brief thought crossed my mind. *Maybe she knows that the TV people come here after a show, and she's deliberately come for that reason.* As our eyes met, she arose and began to make her way toward me. On reaching my side, she stopped and stared down at me for a moment . . . before slapping a book down onto the table, right underneath my nose!

"I want you to know that I had this book in my purse when you were giving me that reading," she stated.

I looked down at the book's cover. It showed a profile drawing of a medieval young man wearing a crown. The title read *The Life of Edward VI*. Of course, my curiosity was piqued and raising my head, I looked questioningly at the woman who stood at my side.

Not waiting for an invitation, she pulled up a chair from the empty table behind ours, placed it next to mine, and with aplomb sat down. She was bubbling over with excitement as if a cork had popped off a bottle of champagne. She then began to tell a tale that attracted the attention of everyone at the table.

"All my life, I've felt that King Edward was my guide," she began. "Whenever I've had to make a decision and didn't know what to do, I've felt as if he were there with me and helping me to make the right choice."

Her exuberance was infectious as she continued her story and everyone was hanging onto her words. For several minutes, she gave details of her lifelong experiences with King Edward's spirit. "I've always known that he's been an influence in my life," she claimed. Every so often, she would pause in her story to thank me profusely for validating what she already instinctively knew. Finally, she came to the end of her narrative. Then, as if she'd suddenly remembered something else, she said "Oh! I forgot to mention that my husband is a politician."

Ding-dong! I almost fell off my chair. For the last ten minutes, this woman's discourse had displayed the same characteristics as that of the Lady in the Court of King Edward. She'd demonstrated that same excitable, impulsive personality and the question that immediately popped into my head was an obvious one. *Could she be repeating the same mistakes in this life?* Was her impulsiveness going to cause an upset in her husband's political career? Was this the reason spirit had used me as a tool to show her the mistakes that she'd made in that previous life and to warn her not to make them again? The chopping off of heads might not be allowed in this day and age—but there are other ways that are just as cruel, if someone wants to destroy a life.

It was obvious from her attitude that she was completely wrapped up in the validation she'd received—but had she understood the importance of the message?

One thing's for certain, I thought sardonically. *She'll be in trouble again if she doesn't get it right this time around.*

This is a perfect example of having to repeat a lesson when we've goofed up in a former life. Remember what I've already told you? When we flunk a grade in school what happens? We have to repeat that grade, of course.

CHAPTER 6

Let's Do Reincarnation!

T he majority of people who have come to see me are seeking answers to life's difficulties. They are looking for direction that will show them the right path to take. Consciously or unconsciously, we all search for tools that will give us the answers we need in our efforts to reach our ultimate goal. Some folks turn to self-help books; some visit a church or temple; others seek counselors, astrologers, tarot card readers, or seers - and some seek me out.

To explain all the dynamics of reincarnation, I'll once again use a car as an analogy. Edgar Cayce said that in dream interpretation a car is symbolic of your body, so it seems appropriate to use this symbol for you in the following:

You are driving your car to a certain place. You know that the fastest route to your destination is to take a particular highway and drive in a certain direction. You're enjoying the scenery as you travel along, and everything is fine until—bam! You've suddenly come upon a barrier across the highway. Those orange cones that indicate roadwork is taking place are stretched across it, and you are forced to stop. The road ahead is closed off. There's a big sign that says "Détour" and an arrow points you off the highway and away from your familiar route. You have absolutely no idea where this detour is going to take you, and you're uncertain as to whether you should follow its lead. What if it takes you away from where you need to be? What should you do? You reluctantly drive away from the highway and go in the direction that the arrow is pointing. Feeling unsure and maybe a little bit out of control, you look for further signs that will give more information, but there's none to be seen. What do you do now?

Life is full of détours, also known as obstacles. You are going along just fine and then wham, you're hit with an unexpected situation that sets you back on your heels. Maybe you lose your job, your spouse hands you divorce papers, or your significant other decides to leaves you. By the way, what are you going to do about that tempting employment position you've been offered in another state? Do you want to uproot your comfortable lifestyle and move into unknown territory? What should you do? Decisions, decisions! You realize that you need to make the right choice, but how can you do that when you don't know what the right choice is? The answer is that you need more information (signposts) that will help you to make the right decision. At this point your guides will usually step in and take over in an attempt to steer you to the right road.

Many of the people to whom I've given readings have this uncertainty in their lives. Choices you make can either be smooth sailing or an uphill battle, depending on how you handle them. Your spirit guides will bend over backward to help you make the right decision and will bring you assistance in many formats. For this reason, they sometimes direct you to my door. And without fail, my Head Honchos will help to reveal a situation in your past life that shows why the present problem in your life has manifested. Just as in this life I had to resolve issues that had been created in Elizabeth's Victorian existence, you too may have unfinished business that you need to complete. That's when your guides and my Head Honchos will step in and use me to assist you.

I've never consciously advertised. My feeling has always been that those who needed my help would be led to me. Of course, metaphysical establishments have advertised whenever they would ask me to give readings for their customers. The same holds true with venues that have invited me for speaking engagements. But even in such environments, folks haven't found me by accident. I'll repeat. There is no such thing as an accident. The following account is a stark example of this point.

Memories of War

During the late 1980s and continuing through to the beginning of the 1990s, I became a frequent guest reader at a very popular metaphysical store. The owner was a savvy business man and was always coming up with some new attraction to entice his customers to spend their money. Consequently he always had a steady stream of folks who came through the door of his shop. One of his most popular attractions was a monthly psychic fair that was always held over a weekend. The place inevitably drew a large crowd as its enthusiastic owner would offer every kind of metaphysical activity to suit all tastes. There were always a couple of tarot card readers, aura readers, runes, Reiki healers'—you name it, and it was there. My own appointment schedule was always full at these affairs.

On a Sunday of one particular weekend, I had back-to-back clients, so that when I eventually got a few minutes' break, I left my assigned small room and headed for the store's main shopping area. In spite of the busy weekend, I wasn't tired but needed to stretch my legs and take a breather. The shop had been chock-full of people for both days, and I was enjoying the upbeat atmosphere of the place. Idly browsing among the stalls full of books, crystals, and New Age baubles that were on display, I lazily glanced around, and for some unknown reason, my focus came to rest on a tall, slim man who stood at the opposite end of the room. He appeared to be taller than the rest of the people and seemed to stand out in the crowd. Two little girls were holding onto his hands. I had no idea why my attention had landed on him, but a feeling that was hard to describe came over me. It was like that feeling one gets when meeting a stranger and the encounter feels familiar, as if you've met before. Know what I mean?

As I continued to meander from one room to another, this man would also be there and would enter my line of vision. I wondered why he kept attracting my attention and shook my head in perplexity.

Switching mental gears, it finally dawned on me that time was passing and there were still clients to see. I glanced at my wrist-watch and did a double take. Time had slipped away from me, and I realized that my next client was due any minute. The man was forgotten as I hurried back to my cubicle in the back of the store.

The rest of the day passed quickly as one person after another visited my little room. Eventually pausing for a few moments, I realized that nobody else was entering, and picking up my client roster, saw that there were no more clients booked. It was time for me to leave. Although the store would remain open for another hour, I'd already made arrangements with Mark (the owner) to leave early as I never liked to stay until closing time. Weekend traffic was heavy in the evening, as people were driving to restaurants or entertainment, and I tried to avoid all the mess of cars on the roads. Grabbing my coat from the coat rack and reaching for my purse from underneath the chair, I headed for the door . . . only to be met by Mark entering.

"Marie. You can't leave yet!" His voice was full of excitement as he pushed the door wide open. "There's a man out front who is insisting that he have a reading from you."

"Really? Why me?" I queried.

"I don't know, but he insists on seeing you!" His voice spoke volumes.

Mark and I were good friends and always accommodated each other, but I was tired and wanted to go home. "Send him to one of the other readers," I said, uncharitably.

"I've already suggested that, but he wants to see you and nobody else." He sounded frustrated. PUH-LEASE!" His hands came together in supplication as he pleaded with me. "He's emphatic. He says he won't leave until he's seen you!"

I wanted to go home, but Mark's obvious predicament was unsettling. I hesitated; flip -flopping between answering yes or no. His imploring face finally got the better of me and heaving a sigh of resignation, I plopped my purse back down and succumbed. Shrugging off my coat and hanging it back on its peg I said, "Okay, send him in. But this is absolutely the last person I'm seeing!"

Within a couple of minutes, the person opened my door and entered. To my surprise, it was the man I'd seen in the store earlier that day. *Has he been here all day?* To be honest, in spite of my reluctance to see him, my curiosity had been aroused when Mark had made his request. I couldn't help but wonder why someone had been so insistent on seeing me when the shop was full of other readers who were eager to use their skills. Now I was more than curious. *This is downright intriguing.*

He stood hesitating in the doorway, and I took this brief moment to size him up. He wasn't as tall as I'd first thought but was still close to six feet, with a loose-limbed stance. Dark brown, well-groomed hair was combed straight back off his high forehead. It looked as neat as if he'd recently had a haircut. His pale-looking face was sharp featured and intense dark eyes looked almost black against the pale complexion. His eyes held my own with a look of expectancy.

Waving a hand toward the empty chair across the table from me, I smiled encouragingly and invited him to sit. "May I ask your name?"

"I'm Alex," he replied. He sat down, stiff and upright as if visiting his dentist's office!

Placing folded arms on the table, I leaned toward him in a relaxed position and gave him my usual introduction. "I don't want you to tell me anything about yourself, Alex, or why you are here," I stated. "The reason for this is because I don't want anything you might tell me to interfere with the sub-conscious thoughts and images that I'll be given."

He nodded his head in understanding, so I continued. "We have many incarnations, but the past life that I'm going to be given for you will be one that is connected to your present life. It will tell you why you have returned again and what you need to be doing at this time." I paused for a moment to allow this to sink in, before continuing. "Also, please don't try to ask questions while I'm relating the information I'll be given, as the space that I'm occupying isn't of this world and if you speak, it feels like a piece of chalk being scratched across a blackboard. It doesn't feel pleasant." I gave him an encouraging smile to soften my words and he relaxed a little.

Following a few more exchanges to allow him to become more comfortable and also to assure myself that he'd understood the directives I'd given, I closed my eyes and cleared my conscious mind . . .

The veil to my sub- conscious rose, and immediately the inner vision produced a scene of what appeared to be a graveyard. Manicured grass formed a foundation for scattered gravestones. The gravestones had a worn, gray appearance in sharp contrast to the neat grass. A few sturdy trees spread their thick branches among the graves . . . a big willow tree shaded the grounds. The place seemed vaguely familiar to me, and I couldn't understand why.

The camera lens of my sub-conscious continued to sweep over the landscape and as I wandered the grounds, the immaculate grass between the headstones seemed to undulate in a breeze. All at once, a strong scent wafted toward me, and I sniffed the air. It was the pungent smell of roses.

I gave a mental jolt of recognition. This was a graveyard in my hometown of England! Mentally shaking my head in bewilderment, I attempted to get rid of the image. *Why are you seeing this? You are not supposed to be seeing anything from your own life. This is ridiculous.* I deliberately tried to shake the image from my sub-conscious, but instead of leaving, the scene just continued to grow stronger, and like a video lens extending, it zoomed in to give a closer view.

The mental camera stopped to focus on an open grave that showed soft dirt piled around its edges. It was obviously a new grave, and flowers were strewn along its sides. Still puzzled but resigned to the fact that it wasn't going to disappear, I waited to see more. For whatever reason, I was obviously meant to see this. The distinctive perfume of roses became more pronounced, and suddenly a childhood memory penetrated my thoughts. I was pulling up a tragic event from my very early childhood.

I barely remember an older sister who died at the age of eighteen. She developed tuberculosis and within six months of the diagnosis, was gone. Childhood memories were vague as far as her funeral was concerned, and I was far too young to grasp the significance of death. But since that time, whenever I smell roses I'm reminded of her funeral. My father operated a popular pub in our town (better known to Americans as a bar), and as the case is in most English pubs, it was a big building that covered most of a city block because the living quarters were attached to it. Prior to her burial, the large entertainment lounge was overflowing with wreaths and bouquets of heavily perfumed flowers, predominantly made up of roses. That room reeked of their scent for ages after it was cleared.

My sub-conscious returned me to this graveyard of my childhood. The past life images were now becoming more defined. They were focusing on the open grave, and I knew that the coffin held a young man's remains.

I realized that this man, Alex, who was sitting and listening to me, was the reincarnated entity of that person in the grave.

His mother stood at the gravesite weeping uncontrollably and was being comforted by other mourners …

The year was 1942. World War II was raging throughout Europe and Hitler's troops had already invaded and subjugated most of Europe. Now, they were concentrating on overpowering England. German armies saturated the shores of Europe, waiting for orders to invade the southern coast of this island nation. The only thing that separated Hitler's soldiers from Britain's mainland was the narrow width of the English Channel and even there, Germans were already occupying tiny islands that sat just ten miles off the English coastline.

The young man in the open grave had died fighting in that war. He had been an air force pilot and history would remember this horrendous time as the Battle of Britain . . .

All at once, the spirit of the dead man was alongside mine and I was reading his thoughts. Waves of anger reverberated from him as he observed his mother's agony. *If I ever return to this world I'll never have children to die in senseless wars. What a waste of life!* The spirit of this entity retained all of his human rage as he left the earth-plane . . .

The images changed and focused on this pilot's death.

Airplanes saturated a cloudless sky, flitting and droning like swarms of angry bees as they turned and dived at each other in mortal combat. The German Luftwaffe and British Royal Air Force were hell-bent on killing each other. A warm summer sun sparkled off steel and glass as aircraft flew through its rays, careening and spinning like a child's yo-yo. Plumes of thick, black smoke marred the clear blue expanse as first one plane was hit by the rat-a-tat-tat of machine guns, then another, and another. Engines screamed in agony as they hurtled out of control and spiraled down to earth, only to burst into flames on impact . . .

Once more the scene changed and was now concentrating on one plane. A young pilot was desperately maneuvering his Spitfire out of the line of enemy fire—but too late. A rain of bullets hit the gallant little fighter plane, puncturing it full of holes. Scorching flames burst from the engine, and within seconds the plane's hood was an inferno. The blaze reeked of burning oil as it swept toward the cockpit, its intense heat blowing out the Plexiglas windshield. The pilot's shock as the flames sprang toward him was too much for his heart to stand, and he was dead before the flames engulfed him. His Spitfire twisted around and around in a ball of fire as it hurtled to the ground . . .

I was returned to the graveside that was now covered in dirt. Wreaths of dead flowers lay on top of it. The headstone on this pilot's grave read that he was nineteen years old. The grave was next to my sister's grave. They had died within days of each other.

This validates what I've already said. We are all connected . . .

Slowly opening my eyes, I returned from this other dimension to the little room in the shop. As usual after a session, I felt as if I were awakening from a vivid dream state. Raising my head, I was met with the piercing stare of the man sitting facing me. Alex's face was expressionless and devoid of even less color than he'd had on entering. We both sat in silence and it seemed like we sat this way for an eternity. When he finally broke the silence, he began a story that I will never forget.

"This is incredible." His voice was full of awe. "To start with, I've been deathly afraid of fire for my entire life and never knew why. Now it all makes sense. But, I have to tell you what made me so compelled to see you." He paused as if he was still collecting his thoughts, and I could see that his past had really impacted him. Inhaling deeply as if he'd been under water and was emerging to take in air, he continued his story.

"This morning, my wife told me that she wanted to come here to have a reading with a tarot card reader who had given her a reading last month. She also wanted me to accompany her as we live ten miles from here and she really doesn't like to drive any distance. I didn't want to as I had more important things to do. I felt exasperated and asked her why she needed another reading when she'd just had one a month ago? She told me in no uncertain terms that I had a choice. Either I could accompany her and watch our girls while she had the reading, or I could stay and babysit them at home. He looked uncomfortable, and I guessed he might be thinking that I considered him to be henpecked. "I gave in," he said. "It seemed easier to bring them to the store to keep them amused than to watch them at home."

His expression turned to one of embarrassment as he continued. "I saw you walking around the shop and for some strange reason, felt drawn to you. It seems so silly to say this, but as I drove my family home, I couldn't shake your image from my mind. I had such a strong feeling that I needed to have a reading with you, and it wouldn't leave. In fact it got stronger as the day progressed. Finally, I couldn't stand it any longer, so gave up and told my wife that I was returning to the shop to see you. She stared at me as if I'd lost my marbles!" He gave a laugh that rang of his mortification. "She reminded me that I hadn't wanted to visit the store with her that morning, so why would I now want to return. There was no logical answer I could give her—so I just left."

He leaned forward in his chair, folded his arms across the table, and searched my face. I could tell that what I'd revealed had really shaken him.

"You've answered so many questions concerning myself that have always puzzled me," he said. "I've always had a tremendous amount of anger built inside me and never known why. Sometimes I explode at those who are the closest to me for the silliest of reasons, and I often wonder why my wife puts up with me!" He hesitated, as if still trying to digest the revelations he'd been given. "I never wanted children. My wife did, so I eventually gave in to her wishes, and we had our two girls. When they were born, my first thought was, thank God they aren't boys, so they'll never have to be killed in a war." He gave an ironic laugh. "Although I don't believe in war, I fought in Vietnam because I had no choice but always knew I wouldn't get killed. Now I know why I was so confident. I'd already lived through that experience!"

He paused, and then concluded his story. "The oddest thing is that my father was an American pilot in WWII."

Was I surprised? No. I know that when we return, we gravitate to that which feels familiar. That's why psychologists call it preconditioning. However; the professionals are usually refering to this life not one from the past.

"What year were you born?" I asked.

"1948," he replied.

I also knew why he'd returned so fast. He needed to finish the contract he'd made that he'd not had time to complete. His life had been cut too short. As I've said, time as we know it doesn't exist. Therefore when a spirit leaves the body before it's accomplished its mission, it returns immediately. Over the years, I've learned via similar situations with clients that this is a fact whenever a life has been inadvertently interrupted. It's like driving over a nail and having to stop to change the flat tire before we can continue with our journey. And the sooner we can fix the problem, the better! However, in the spirit world, the amount of time this project has taken is probably only a few seconds.

• • • ● ● ● • •

I've never seen this man again, but feel sure that because he had the satisfaction of knowing where he'd come from and why he was here, he'd know how to finish this particular chapter in his life. Hopefully, he would seek professional help to learn how to control his anger. I'm sure, however, that whether he did or didn't, it was a big release for him to have learned that the situation that had caused the anger no longer existed. This knowledge would certainly aid in his healing. And he would hopefully be able to enjoy a better relationship with his wife.

Observing his grave next to my sister's grave had also impacted my own psyche. It gave me a sense of closure to her life as I'd been much too young to understand the loss at the time of her death. This illustrates one of the many times when I've given 10 percent of myself and gained so much more in return. Once again, the realization came to me as to how perfectly uniform the universe is in conducting our lives. Alex and I were meant to meet in this life-time to mutually resolve known and unknown issues that we both had. This was one of those "detours" in our individual journeys that we both had been hesitant to follow. And the detours had turned out to be more advantageous to our spiritual growth than the road our free will would have chosen to travel.

This is what is meant by letting go and letting God. When necessary, allow spirit to deviate you from your chosen path. If your freewill is steering you too far away from your spiritual growth and you start to feel stuck, you'll be given plenty of help in untying those tangled knots.

Incidentally, and on a personal note, the spirit of this sister stays close to me and is one of my personal guides.

By the way, as an afterthought for you to consider, I'd like to leave you with this thought. Linear time is a man-made concept. Therefore, if every past event and those in the future are happening at this very moment, could it be that the reason Alex and I both felt we knew each other when we met, was because at this same moment in time we were together in 1942 at that gravesite? Mind-boggling, isn't it?

• • • ● ● ● ● • •

Hitler's Admirer

Dixie had been my hairdresser for two or three years. Apart from being great at what she did, she was a nice person with a generous heart that showed in her smile and outgoing personality. While sitting in her chair as she made me presentable, we'd exchange small talk and catch up on each other's lives.

One day, a friend needed a good hairdresser, and I recommended Dixie. She liked the hairdo that Dixie gave her and so, she continued to visit her salon. Sometime later, as I sat in Dixie's booth, I got an unexpected surprise. Instead of immediately beginning her ministrations on my locks, she stood unmoving, staring at my reflection in her mirror. She stood poised like the Statue of Liberty, except with a comb and scissors held high in one hand instead of a torch. Her expression was odd.

I patted the top of my head to make sure I'd not sprouted horns. "What's wrong?

"You didn't tell me you believe in reincarnation."

Her statement threw me for a loop, and for a moment I sat gaping at her mirror image. Stalling to answer directly, I asked, "Where did that come from?"

Apparently, on my friend's previous visit to her salon, she'd discussed my paranormal beliefs and metaphysical thoughts with Dixie. Now, she wanted to know more.

I was still taken aback because although I'd known her for some time, I'd never broached the subject of reincarnation during our conversations. As I've already explained, I've learned to be discreet in discussing anything of a paranormal nature with people that don't share my credence, and Dixie had never given me any reason to think she might have the same beliefs. I definitely do not discuss reincarnation with someone I don't know, as many people are either uncomfortable with the subject or in extreme cases, feel that I'm being blasphemous. One time, a dear old lady went so far as to tell me she would pray for my soul after she learned of my sinful thoughts!

Dixie and I had always had a good rapport, but our chats usually consisted of bits of gossip or ordinary events in our lives. This new revelation was indeed a surprise, especially when she started to share her own metaphysical beliefs with me. She began by relating one particular paranormal occurrence that she'd experienced.

"When I was a little girl, my folks drove to this town that we'd never been to before, but I saw the outside of a house and knew what it looked like inside. I knew I'd lived in that house in a previous life. My folks accused me of having a vivid imagination and told me to behave myself!"

As she performed her usual ministrations to my hair, we got into a deep discussion of reincarnation, and I found that we were very much in accord in our perceived realities. When she'd finished doing her thing, she asked me if I would give her a past life reading. We made arrangements for me to visit her home on her next day off from work.

A few days later, we were sitting facing each other at her dining room table. After a few minutes of comfortable small talk, I gave her my usual instructions and cleared my mind of any outside distractions.

Before I begin to relate Dixie's past, I need to share with you something that sometimes occurs when I'm being introduced to a previous incarnation. Occasionally I get an image that alerts me to the kind of life that's about to appear; that is, it will show me a scene that gives an idea of the kind of energy produced in that life. Its purpose is to let me know as to whether it will be a sad or light-hearted past life; heavy-duty, or nonsensical. It's as if I'm sitting in a theater's audience and listening to the orchestra playing the overture that introduces the show. If the past life is going to be light-hearted, the introduction will be as if I'm about to see a Broadway musical. You'll know what I mean if you've ever attended such a show. The overture will usually reprise its musical content and is very up-beat. But if the reading is to be a serious drama, the music will reflect this with its somber overtones. Hence I call this introductory scene an Overture.

The atmosphere became still as we both silently waited to see what would occur ...

I was now receiving one such overture and it was far from pleasant. An image of the Devil appeared in front of my inner vision, gyrating in a satanic dance. His flaming red eyes stared at me while his barbed tail swung back and forth. The image reminded me of the opera *Faust*.

The Devil made a vow. "She'll never get away from me no matter what happens. NEVER!"

This brief introduction ended, and the "play" began . . .

I was taken to Salem, Massachusetts. It was during that terrible time that was to become known as the Salem witch trials. At that time, the entity now known as Dixie was married to a God-fearing, Bible-thumping minister, but she was not of the same nature. This wife was an independent-minded woman who enjoyed practicing all the things that her puritanical husband condemned as evil, such as reading books that were not the Bible. She enjoyed dancing and cavorting in a way that was not becoming to a woman, instead of being compliant and subdued as a wife should be. In his eyes she was acting ungodly as she was outgoing, friendly, and spoke her mind without any thought to her reputation. This minister's wife was a strong-minded woman married to a narrow-minded man who thought women should be seen and not heard. And heaven forbid she refused to obey her husband's wishes!

My friend, you know what such a man would be called in today's world, don't you? To put it mildly he was a complete chauvinistic control freak.

Once again, the scene changed, and I was seeing a blazing bonfire in a town square. A body was bound to a stake at the top of the bonfire. This husband was so enraged at his inability to control his wife that he used his role as a minister to influence the town's authorities into believing her to be a witch. He'd convinced them that she needed to be purified of her sins by burning her at the stake. Yet, even as the flames consumed the woman's body, she refused to repent her so-called wickedness. The frustrated and enraged husband repeated the Devil's vow:

"She'll never get away from me."

I was told that this minister was once again in Dixie's life but was now in a female body.

As the vision faded, I returned to the present and adjusted to the surroundings of Dixie's dining room. It was such a pleasure to see the sun shining through the room's windows after seeing this horror from the past.

Observing her expression as she sat with me at her table, I saw the same incredulity that I'd seen so often on clients' faces after having had a previous life revealed. She stood up and said, "I want to show you something."

With that, she left the dining area and opened a closet door that was in a small hallway between the dining room and kitchen entrance. My eyes followed her as she reached up to its high shelf and pulled down a box. As I watched her digging through it, I sat wondering what she was planning on showing me. After a scant minute, she gave an exclamation of satisfaction and came away from her search with a framed picture in her hand. I couldn't see the picture in the frame until she brought it to the table and handed it to me. I was holding an eight-by-seven-inch, black and white photograph of a young child and a man in a military uniform. She was looking up with adoration at this man in the uniform. The uniform had a swastika emblazoned on the shirt. The man was bending toward the little girl with a benevolent smile on his face to receive a bunch of flowers she was offering to him. The man was Adolf Hitler. The picture held my gaze for a few seconds, and then I raised questioning eyes to look at Dixie.

"That's my mother," she stated. "She was born and raised in Nazi Germany."

Dixie proceeded to explain. Her mother was born at the time when Adolf Hitler had just come into power, and she was five years old when the picture was taken. It was at the beginning of his infamous regime that was a precursor to WWII. This child, who was now her mother, had grown into an adult during the war, and when allied troupes had eventually conquered Germany, she met and married an American G.I.—Dixie's father. At the time of their marriage, the mother was seventeen.

Dixie began a confession. "All my life, my mother has been emotionally abusive to me. It was so bad that at one point I saw a counselor for the problems she was causing in my life." She continued to tell of the entire emotional trauma she'd suffered as a child at the hands of her bullying mother. "You should see her house. It's full of Nazi mementos," she concluded.

Not only had this overbearing woman controlled Dixie's life, but she shared with me that her mild-mannered father was also a submissive victim to this woman's control.

Of course, her mother had played the role of domineering husband to his wife (now Dixie) in that earlier life, but the woman was now enjoying a double whammy. She could also have the pleasure of bullying her husband.

A few months after the reading, Dixie told me that she'd had the courage to confide the story of her unhappy childhood to her father. She was still too afraid to confront her mother. Apparently, her father was clueless as to his wife's behavior toward their daughter but talking to him did help Dixie to heal.

As always, the universe had provided Dixie with an answer to this emotionally charged relationship between daughter/wife and mother/husband. Now that she knew the cause, she could begin to resolve this negative bond.

This past life story is one that I've had the satisfaction of seeing resolved. Dixie has long since retired from her hairdressing work, but she's one of those people who have remained in my life. We don't see each other very often, but we always have a lot to talk over when we do. Her father has passed, but her mother is now in her nineties and suffering from dementia. I don't know what circumstances brought about the change in their relationship, but Dixie tells me that her mother is a much nicer person in her senile old age. She regrets her actions toward her daughter and according to Dixie, all is forgiven. They now enjoy a bonding that should have happened a long time ago, but better late than never.

• • • ● ● ● ● • •

Gotcha!

Two women sat on my living room sofa. One of them was a previous client and this time she'd brought a friend to my house for a reading. The former client was in her mid-fifties and her friend looked to be the same age, but this is where the similarities ended as they were as different as night and day. I remembered the previous visitor as being a quiet, reserved woman and although she had a nice personality, she wouldn't stand out in a crowd. In contrast, her partner's outgoing mannerisms dominated the room and exuded a strong energy. She'd started a conversation almost immediately after entering and hadn't stopped talking since! But I liked the woman, in spite of her unrestrained persona. As I watched her from my seat across the room and listened to her chatter, I took this time to give her a discreet once-over.

Her eyes were reminiscent of a gray winter's morning and showed frank curiosity as she stared into mine. She wore gray-rimmed spectacles that emphasized the color of her eyes while expertly dyed brown hair framed a carefully made up face. A brush of silver shadow swept across her eyelids and a thick coating of mascara flushed out the eyelashes. She'd tastefully applied a hint of coral lipstick to well-shaped lips. *She was probably a beauty in her younger days,* I thought. And she still knew how to set-off her best assets to advantage. *Including her self-confidence, but will she ever stop talking?*

Her accent sounded as if she was from the East Coast, which was confirmed when she told me she was originally from Brooklyn. Her over-the-top personality seemed to be as natural as breathing, but I'd long since learned this to be a characteristic of most folks from New York City. Having once lived across the river from Manhattan, I knew that the people there are not averse to asking personal questions, but the appearance of rudeness is offset by their disarming friendliness. There were times when I missed this New York open friendliness, and this lady seemed to be a good example of that quality, even if gregarious in her enthusiasm. Unfortunately, she was in complete control of the conversation, and time was wasting. I needed to get a hold on the situation. Thankfully, as I was just wondering if she would ever let me get on with her reading, she paused long enough for me to get a word in, and I quickly brought the conversation around to the reason why they were here.

"Let's go to my dining room where I have my recorder set up," I said and pointedly arose to head away from the living room. Taking this as their cue to follow, the women arose, and I led the way to empty chairs around my dining room table. I placed the recorder in front of myself and settled down to business.

Once she was relaxed and both were settled, I began my usual introduction, really emphasizing the standard affirmation that she wasn't to say anything while being given her past life information. "If you speak it will feel like you're gate crashing."

Her friend was no problem as she already knew the routine and had remained mostly silent since entering my house. Anyway, the woman from Brooklyn got the message and nodding her head in understanding, made a sweeping hand motion to zip her lips!

Immediately on entering that no man's land where time doesn't exist, I felt myself to be in a heavy, dark place. A sense of unrest and frustration seemed to surround me . . .

The air felt hot and sticky with humidity, and I was given the information that I was in India. This climate that was encompassing me seemed to be symbolic of the Indian energy at this particular time in history—mid-1800. Crowds began to appear in this timeless space and were frantically scurrying back and forth as if they didn't know where to go. There was a sense of urgency permeating this Asian subcontinent . . .

Queen Victoria was on the British throne and India was known as the crown jewel of all the British colonies. With its millions of inhabitants, this vast country was the reigning glory of the British Empire. Britain had ruled

India since the 1600s, and when I say ruled, England's overseers dominated the people with a superior attitude that conveyed a sense of their own importance over the lives of India's people. They controlled with cruelty more often than not, as India's citizens were expected to be subservient to British rule. Indian household servants were treated well by the elite as long as they remembered to stay in their proper place in the pecking order of British society, but lowly citizens were treated as nonentities. And it didn't help that the caste system among India's subjects was also prevalent.

Unrest among India's people had been rising for some time, and the British governing body seemed to think that the only way to subdue it was to increase their oppressive laws and regulations. Their superior attitude only added fuel to the fire of resentment. Consequently, the citizens had begun to balk at this unfair situation, and frustration had flowered into angry confrontations. Physical violence was increasing.

These were unsettling times in this vast nation and the simmering pot was about to boil over ...

A young Indian man entered my vision. He was neither subservient nor ignorant, and he was passionate in his hatred of the British. If this had been the time of Gandhi's fight for independence, he'd have supported and protected this great man with his own life. As it was, he was the instigator and leader of one of the many rioters fighting against those hated English settlers. Homes were burned to the ground, and gangs of Indian marauders slaughtered British families. In retaliation, the authorities imprisoned and tortured any Indian that was caught. The British were having a hard time putting a stop to the uprisings, and clashes between the rioters and the ruling forces became a daily occurrence. Suffice it to say that the situation was worse than that infamous Boston Tea Party that led to the fight for America's independence.

As my sub-conscious took in these scenes of revolt, it became focused on the Indian leader of this particular riot. He was amidst a desperate fight with the British military, but the brave Indians were no match for their enemy's rifles. The leader suddenly felt an excruciating pain in his chest. He had been shot through the heart and was dead before he hit the ground, but as his spirit left his body, he died with all the fury and hatred he felt toward the British …

Of course, this 1800s Indian rebel was now occupying the body of the woman from Brooklyn.

The scenes vanished into that distant past and I was returned to the present timeline. The woman across the table from me was sitting with a blank expression on her face. She seemed to be in a state of shock and for once, she didn't have anything to say!

Her laid-back friend finally broke the silence and turning to address her, she said, "See, I told you!" Her tone sounded triumphant.

This woman who had displayed such self-confidence on entering my home didn't respond, then after what seemed to be an eternity, she leaned toward me across the table, as if to emphasize her words. She said, "You're not going to believe this."

Try me, I thought.

"For the past ten years, I've been living with an Englishman."

I had a hard time smothering the laughter that arose in my throat. *The universe certainly has a sense of humor when it comes to payback time!* The spirits in charge of her destiny had even gone as far as choosing me, a British woman, to deliver her this problematic message!

She told a long and complicated story of her relationship with this significant other, and what a story it was! It sounded like she was on an endless roller coaster ride; up-and-down, swerving recklessly this way and that, feeling the thrill of the ride but scared as the coaster climbed upward to the next peak, knowing that when it reached the top it would plunge her into a freefall.

"He knows exactly how to push my buttons," she said with exasperation in her voice, "He can get me so mad I could spit nails!"

I had to bite my tongue to stop myself from making a caustic comment. *So what else is new?* It also crossed my mind that her significant other could be the British soldier who had shot her in that Indian life. *Whatever, it's all part of the master plan.*

This was the epitome of a love/hate relationship; the hate carried over from that Indian experience.

From the description of this Englishman's personality, he sounded as if he was a very laid-back individual because she let me know that whenever she blew up at him, he would calmly take it in stride, causing her even more irritation.

"I love him but he can make my blood boil and it's as if he enjoys doing it!"

Of course he does! Her struggle with hate was as hot and humid as that Indian climate, and the rage she felt from that former battle with the British was still prevalent. She couldn't live with him, and she couldn't live without him.

It was very obvious to me (as I'm sure it is to you) why they were together. He was the catalyst that was forcing her to learn a lesson. She needed to resolve her feelings of hatred. Hate causes wars, and we all know that wars devastate our lives. She'd already lost her life once due to the conflict between India and Britain. Did she want to lose it again in a more personal war? War is not just unproductive, it's tragic and senseless to individuals as well as to countries, but the worst damage it causes is to a person's spiritual progress. It's a crushing blow.

She needed to learn the meaning of forgiveness and also unconditional love. My client was been offered the opportunity to get rid of her hatred via the most intimate relationship a human can experience—the relationship between lovers. And an Englishman, no less!

I couldn't help but smile at the irony of the curve she'd been thrown by the universe. Gathering chaff instead of wheat took on a whole new meaning.

I would like to have seen her lover's past life, but it didn't really matter as the message she'd been given was all about her. And it was a foregone conclusion that if she didn't get it right this time, you know what would happen, don't you? Of course, she'd come back and do it again.

Incidentally, she shared with me that her doctor had told her that she had a weak heart. She'd obviously returned with a damaged heart caused by the shot from that soldier's gun. I thought to myself, *Lady. You have a heart problem in more ways than one.*

· · ● ● ● ● ● · ·

A Native American

One of the advantages of having the gift of sight is that it's widened my perspective of history. I love history, but most books on the subject give only dry facts. However, whenever I'm given insight into a client's previous life, I also get a better perspective of history; how certain periods of time have influenced an individual that in turn has influenced the actions of society. In other words, by having the privilege of seeing how a specific timeline has affected a client's life, my historical knowledge has become more meaningful.

The following Native American lifetime is a prime example of historical events beyond the narrow scope of history books. It's an account of one individual's gifts that were enhanced due to historical events and then honed after the entity returned in this lifetime.

As you know, the original residents of the U.S.A. were known as Indians, but in today's climate, it's considered politically correct to give them the title of Native Americans. The fact is that by whatever name a race of people are presently known, whenever I'm given a past life, I am given the client's name that is used during that particular time in history. This same reasoning applies to a country when it's had a name change. Example: I had a client that lived during the fourteenth century in a country known at that time as Siam. In our present century, he would be known as a citizen of Thailand and therefore not Siamese. Such was the case with the following past life story of an Indian/Native American incarnation.

During the years when I was travelling to various states to give talks and readings, I was asked to present a lecture on reincarnation at a well-known metaphysical establishment in Tucson, Arizona. As per usual, the talk was followed by requests for private readings, and the following encounter occurred at that store.

The woman who sat facing me looked to be in her mid-forties. Tall and slim with clear blue eyes and perfectly coifed, blond hair, she appeared to be full of self-confidence. She sat across from me completely at ease as she waited for a reading. As always, I explained that we have many incarnations, but the life I would encounter would disclose the reason for her return at this time, and I soon found out that in her case, she'd returned to continue the job she'd had in a previous life as an Indian medicine man/healer.

At first, I thought the image that immediately appeared was one of those familiar overtures that sometimes introduce the action that is to follow. However, this time the opening introduction was personally familiar to me, and I knew that it was not an overture, but a fact.

The woman was surrounded by a circle of close-knit spirits who stood with arms linked around each other. This circle encompassed her as if in support and protection. The reason that it was familiar to me was because I had seen such a circle surrounding myself after the passing of my husband and my consequent struggle to get through the grieving process. Spirits of departed relatives and folks I had known in this life had formed a protective, encircling barrier that safeguarded me. They had stayed and protected me in their loving safety as long as I had needed their support.

At this moment, I didn't know why such a circle was protecting this client but didn't question their appearance. For whatever reason, they were there because she apparently needed their spiritual strength, and she needed to know this.

Know this my friend, because it's important for you to realize this fact. If you ever find yourself in a place of intolerable emotional pain, especially after losing a loved one, you will always have this same protection. You are never alone without support. I call it the Circle of Love.

The time period that I had entered was during North America's early years of occupation by the White Man . . .

As the image of the circle faded away, it was replaced by a scene from this earlier time in America's history. I was given a portrait of a strong and forceful Indian man. His energy was as steady and as luminous as the setting sun that blazed on the horizon behind his head, and this brilliant, setting sun seemed to symbolize the decline of the Native American way of life. I was seeing a representation of the Native Americans' indomitable spirit and fortitude as they faced their waning power.

I knew that this client, now sitting and listening to me, had been from a large tribe of southwestern Indians. Yet, the entity was more than a healer for his people. He was an acknowledged Seer, and all his people, from the chieftain down to every child, valued his wisdom that was practical as well as spiritual.

I realized that his energy that emanated from him was once again in this woman. This energy reminded me of Abraham Lincoln's or Winston Churchill's vigorous individualism and leadership. The Indian loved his native land and its people and was willing to die if necessary to protect them. Being a Sensitive (a person with second sight), he foresaw the White Man's continual and increasing betrayal toward his people, and although many of their tribes had already suffered, he knew that their suffering would grow in intensity. Apart from having their land taken away from them, the biggest catastrophe was their loss of dignity and pride. Their heritage was being crushed and their native rights taken away.

This medicine man knew that he couldn't change what was foretold, but he did what he could to protect his people and soften the blow. He felt sad and frustrated, realizing that his people couldn't fight the White Man's strength of numbers. The only thing he could do was to prepare the people and help them to sustain their inner strength and spiritual light. Even as he watched his people being downtrodden, he knew that their generational, inherited spirituality could not be obliterated, no matter what was inflicted upon their bodies . . .

This woman who sat listening to me and absorbing her past life had returned once again with those same qualities. The past life personality had been powerful and effective, and so she'd returned to display and utilize this gift in the same manner.

Eventually the story ended, and as I returned to the present-day reality, I saw by the woman's body language that she was already aware of what I'd revealed. I was only validating this past life for her personal satisfaction. She then proceeded to share with me accounts of her present life that seemed to parallel that of her Indian past.

"My husband is a Navaho Indian," she began quietly.

As she started to relate the life she was leading, I realized why she'd returned at this particular time in history. She'd chosen this century as it was a new beginning for the Indian nations of America. They were now returning to their rightful place in this land and would no longer be subservient. And the Native Americans were more than willing to work hard to regain what they had lost. This entity had returned to support and assist her people in this endeavor, and the timing was now right.

As the woman shared her life with me, it became obvious that she was continuing the job she'd performed in the past. She was dedicating her time to do volunteer work for indigent Native Americans, and at the same time healing their shattered self-esteem. Although she was modest about her work, it was obvious to me that she was still showing that same strong sense of compassion that she was revered for in that former lifetime. As she recounted her story, it became clear that many Native Americans depended upon her for their welfare and lawful rights. She was performing the number one task that we all return to accomplish but sometimes forget to do, that is to help our fellow man whenever we can and by whatever means we are able.

After completing her story, she gave me a final piece of personal information.

"I have cancer."

Ah! That's why I had seen the protective circle. She wholeheartedly agreed with me when I shared my belief that they were her support team and thanked me for verifying that which she already sensed. Not only had the reading validated her preordained mission, but had also confirmed for her that she was not alone in dealing with this dreadful disease. Angels were with her.

Whenever I think of this woman, I wonder if she survived her illness. But, whether she did or not I'm sure of one thing, she would once again leave her mark with her people before she left. And I'm guessing that wherever she is, she's satisfied to see that the Native Americans are finally getting back their dignity and able to own their inheritance. Her life also reminds me that even those entities that are a strong and powerful force need an occasional, encouraging hug.

· ● ◉ ◉ ◉ ◉ ● ·

Atonement

At the end of the 1980s, I was asked to conduct a monthly workshop for a group of folks who were interested in learning more about reincarnation. At that time, many people were still just opening up to this belief system and eager to expand their thinking. They were ready to explore their metaphysical/spiritual horizons.

It was held at a small bookstore in the community where I was living, and the owner of the store (she was a personal friend) had made the suggestion after running the idea by her customers. It was gladly accepted by eager attendees, and each month, they would fill the empty room in the back of the little store. The format was simple. Via a series of specific mental exercises and by relating factual events, I would lead them into thinking outside the box so they could use their own sub- conscious abilities. All I had to do was to open the sub-conscious part of their minds. To bring them to an awareness of their powerful sub consciousness, I'd end the workshop by demonstrating a past life reading for one of the attendees.

On one particular evening, there were around a dozen people in attendance and it was the first visit for the woman I selected for a reading. During the workshop her energy had impacted mine, and I felt a strong urge to choose her for my closing demonstration. It seemed as if my Head Honchos were pushing me into this.

She sounded unsure of herself when I suggested she be my recipient, but nevertheless agreed to it. She looked to be in her forties. Her dress was in the hippie style of the sixties, as she wore an ankle length cotton skirt that sported large red and yellow flowers on a black background. A white T-shirt showed under a short denim jacket, and the latter looked as if it had seen better days. Although it was mid-winter, she wore open, strapped sandals.

I asked her if she felt comfortable at having a reading heard by the other people, but emphasized that I would be discreet. Naturally I didn't want to share anything from it that might cause her embarrassment. But I also knew that if I wasn't to speak of a particular incident, I'd be warned not to go there.

The woman didn't hesitate and nodded her head in acceptance.

"Will you tell me your name?"

She offered the information that her name was Vivian, "But folks call me Viv," she added in a friendly manner.

"Hi Viv. I hope you've enjoyed the evening in my witch's parlor," I said jokingly; wanting to make sure that the atmosphere wasn't heavy duty. It was a good move, as everyone laughed and visibly relaxed.

Per usual, I explained the dynamics of the reading for benefit of the other people as well as Vivian, and used this time to observe the woman more thoroughly. It struck me that she radiated vitality. Her features were nondescript, except for expressive, dark eyes that reflected a sense of serenity. Personally I think of the eyes as being windows to the soul.

Finishing the introduction, I ended with the admonition that was always the most important. "Please don't tell me anything about your life as I don't want my conscious self to retain anything you might reveal. Naturally, after the reading, you may share your thoughts with everyone if you wish, and ask anything you want."

She nodded in understanding and seemed eager for me to begin.

As I closed my eyes, the room and its people began to disappear, and I deliberately blanked out my surroundings as mists of time swirled around inside my head . . .

My alternate self entered a dark place, and a sense of foreboding swept through my body.

I gave a mental shudder as an ominous cloud swirled around me, and I felt reluctant to move forward. Yet, hesitating wasn't an option. I knew that whatever I was meant to see was for this entity's welfare, besides which, my

Head Honchos always protected me and would never allow me to experience personal danger when in an altered state.

A midnight sky was as black as pitch without benefit of either moonlight or stars. I stood in a country meadow and smelled the sweetness of damp grass ... something rustled in the undergrowth ... then quiet once more ...

Suddenly, I saw flickering lights in the distance, and they were moving toward me. Nervously, I watched as the lights continued to move closer and become stronger. After a few moments, I could make out the shadowy figures of roughly a dozen cloaked people, moving purposely in my direction. My instinct was to run, but I knew that I couldn't because my body wasn't present—just my spirit. As they came to a stop within a few yards of where I stood, I could see that the glowing lights were coming from blazing torches that were held high in the air by their outstretched arms. The figures stood in formation, frozen in time. Unmoving, they faced me as if challenging my presence.

With a sense of shock, I took in their clothing. Each wore identical smocks that covered their entire bodies and shone ghostly white in the light from the torches. I couldn't see their faces as they were hidden by white, conical shaped hoods that covered their entire heads and faces. Through black slits in the hoods, I knew that piercing eyes were studying me. Ah yes dear reader, you've probably guessed who they were. I was in the presence of the Ku Klux Klan. The meadow I was standing in was situated in the Deep South ...

The American Civil War had just ended with the North's victory and complete devastation was in the Southern states. Grand-looking plantations were ransacked and in rubble while fields were no longer fertile. Slaves were free of their masters, and many of them wandered the countryside, not knowing what to do or where to go. President Lincoln's well-intentioned idea of giving them freedom hadn't taken into consideration their overall welfare after leaving their owners. The majorities of them were born into slavery and knew no other life than being owned by the plantations.

My sub-conscious had landed me amidst the turmoil of this time in a divided country. To add to the devastation, the Ku Klux Klan was systematically searching out the terrified former slaves and subjecting them to their atrocities. This particular group that stood facing me was having a field day!

There's no reason for me to go into detail regarding the cruelty of these times as history has well documented the Ku-Klux-Klan's agenda. No wonder I felt such fear to be so close to this group of its members!

What was more shocking was to realize that this innocent-seeming woman, who was listening to me, was a member of those white-clad figures facing me in that meadow.

The group remained where they were. I knew that they really weren't a threat to me, only toward the former slaves that they were seeking. My conscious mind began to fight to get back to the reality of the bookstore and finally, with a sense of relief, I found myself returning...

Still feeling the negativity from that former time, I opened my eyes and looked apprehensively for this woman's reaction to this life that she'd lived. Would she feel offended? Was she perhaps embarrassed or upset by the cruelty of the role she had played? Even more significant, did she now regret having given permission to have this life made public to the rest of the attendees?

Vivian was sitting as calm as a cucumber. *Does she understand how infamous these people were and that she was one of them?*

"How do you feel regarding this former life that's just been exposed to you?" My voice sounded tentative to my own ears as I asked the question, trying to gauge what her reaction would be. Everyone else remained quiet and still. All eyes were on Viv.

She spoke. "It makes perfect sense to me." A sad little smile was on her face, but the tone of her voice sounded calm. "I feel relieved as I've had so many puzzling questions on my mind that I couldn't answer. You've just answered them."

Viv told her story as everyone listened. There was a sense of awe among the participants as she opened up her life story.

"For many years, I've been a foster parent to neglected and traumatized children. But what has puzzled me is the fact that I've always felt this dire need to take into my home African American children. I've never taken care of a white child because I felt that they didn't need me as much as these other children did. I feel terrible when a child has to leave me and move on." At this point her demeanor became lighter, and she really smiled. "But I did adopt a baby who was born addicted to drugs. His teenage mother was an abuser. He had multiple problems that he had to overcome, mental as well as physical, but he's now five years old and much better, thank goodness, and I love him to pieces!

Fears of negative reactions from her companions left my thoughts. Each face in the room full of listeners displayed a look of respect and admiration.

After the group had left and I sat in the empty room, I contemplated this special woman's life and compared it to that previous incarnation. She was most certainly paying back a karmic debt, and I'd like to bet that because of her endeavors, she'd skipped a grade toward her graduation! It also reiterated the absolute power of spirit. When we get out of the way of our ego and allow spirit to take over, it's amazing what we can accomplish in our life

I'm certain that the people attending that meeting would also go home with a much wider knowledge of what reincarnation is all about. They would understand the full meaning of what paying karmic debts really entails— unconditional love.

Answers

By this time, my friend, you've probably got the gist of how reincarnation works. Even though you may not consciously be aware of why you are following a certain style of living, at a sub- conscious level you do know. As the personal events I've related have shown you, every single detail of a person's past is recorded. Some folks call these details the Akashi records. The following is a statement that I've repeated before but will repeat again because it's so important.

We don't only inherit the DNA of our parents, we also return with the DNA from past life experiences.

We may return with certain physical ailments and/or emotional or mental issues because our personality carries forward traits, both positive and negative, from past experiences. A prime example of these inherited emotional and physical characteristics is the woman who hated the British. She'd returned carrying hatred for the British race. And had also died from a bullet wound to the heart; hence she'd returned with a weak heart. In contrast, Viv sub-consciously knew what she had to do in this life even though she wasn't consciously cognizant of it. It didn't matter because she'd replaced hate with unconditional love.

Physical ailments are the most visible detail that we bring back. I'm not saying that every illness we experience is a foregone conclusion, but we do seem to feel comfortable bringing with us ailments that we've previously carried. At a subtler level, we return with mental or emotional traumas, such as the wartime pilot's death from shock at the fire's encroachment toward him. His return with a fear of fire was a foregone conclusion. He'd also left this earth plane having such a strong sense of anger at his demise that he carried the anger issues with him when he returned. Anger is a real biggie in the overall scheme of things.

Vivian's past life compared to her present role is a very good example of going the extra mile in resolving so-called sins from the past. Although we may not consciously realize that this is what we're doing, at a spiritual level we do know. She was fulfilling the contract that she'd made prior to returning and had really lived up to its commitment.

The following brief snippets I'm now going to give you are further examples that emphasize the dynamics of reincarnation. They show how each carat of life is so perfectly created to form that diamond. The spirit, the mind, and the body are each individually taken into consideration so that each lifetime experience fits into the Oneness of All That Is.

George was a gentleman of quiet demeanor; listening with full attention as I relayed a past that was significant to his present. Amazingly, he had acted as a "gopher" (servant) to that genius named Leonardo De Vinci. He was a young lad of the streets, and the artist took him under his wing not only to attend to the mundane tasks of cleaning his brushes and palettes, but also to teach the boy his unique, artistic techniques. At the same time, the boy also absorbed De Vinci's engineering skills. Personally, this reading gave me an insight into this artist's caring and unselfish nature. Not only was he a genius, but he apparently shared his gifts unselfishly with those less talented than himself.

After the reading, George told me that he was an engineer by profession, but he loved to paint and wished he could concentrate more on his art. But with a family to support, he needed to earn a steady income. Even though his salary as an engineer was pretty good, his heart was really into being an artist. Of course, he'd inherited the engineering skills from the life under Da Vinci's tutelage as well as retaining the artistic skills that the man had taught him. Unfortunately, as a mere gopher, he had returned with a lack of self confidence in his abilities as an artist.

The reading was telling him to take a plunge and paint as many pretty pictures as he could imagine! He needed to trust his self-worth, and the rest would fall into place. He probably wasn't a budding art genius, but he did need to enjoy his artistic gift. If we don't take a chance with ourselves, how do we know what we can accomplish with our talents?

One day, I was wandering around a metaphysical store, and a very pretty girl passed by me and drew my attention with a jolly, "Hi, Marie." I had no clue as to who she was and felt duly embarrassed. I might add that this has happened to me on numerous occasions when former clients have greeted me, but it's hard for me to remember everyone with whom I've come in contact. Seeing my lack of recognition, the girl said cheerfully "I'm the concubine!"

Now I remembered. The girl had an effervescent personality that radiated a love for life. I guessed her age to be in the late twenties. She'd sought me out at one of those psychic fairs and had entered my room loaded with an abundance of energy.

Her former life, which was connected to her present, had taken place in ancient Japan. I remembered her as being a concubine to a very rich merchant. She was part of his harem and regularly at his command whenever he chose to order her to his bed.

This man was cruel as well as rich, and his sexual appetite required several such concubines, but he'd soon become tired of ordering the same one to oblige his needs. And so, whenever he became bored with one of his girls, he would send her out to the streets to fend for her own self as best as she could. If she really displeased him, he would have her killed. Therefore, as his concubine, this former client had become very adept at saving her own life. She was very shrewd and smart, and each time she felt her master's interest waning, she would re-invent herself. She'd find new ways to entice and manipulate this man so that she'd insure her safety. By learning to keep his sexual interest alive, he would continue to keep her around for his pleasure. Needless to say, this concubine was always in fear for her own life.

This young woman had shared with me that she'd had many boyfriends but never married and had no intention of doing so. "Don't get me wrong," she'd said. "I like men, but when they start to get serious, I dump 'em!"

She'd sub- consciously returned with a big dose of fear. From her former experiences, she was preconditioned into thinking that intimacy meant death, and self–preservation was her constant companion. Until she let go of her fear and learned to trust, she'd never have a fulfilling relationship with anyone, especially men.

The following is a good example of a recurring physical condition. The woman who sat before me said she was a housewife and introduced herself as Teresa. She'd spent a previous life as a Canadian mountaineer in the wilderness of that country. He was used to being alone and in fact, enjoyed the solitude. Unfortunately, he broke one of his legs, and because he was so far away from civilization, he had to set it himself. For the rest of that life he walked with a decided limp and always felt its throbbing ache.

Teresa shared with me that she had a permanent rod in one of her legs because of an accident earlier in her life. This wasn't the reason for the reading, but it does demonstrate very clearly how we feel the need to bring physical ailments with us when we return. In her former life, Teresa had learned to live with her incapacitating accident. The outcome was that she felt comfortable with this situation and consequently had a preconditioned need to return and repeat the same physical handicap.

A girl named Laura had met her end by drowning in her former life. She confessed that in her present life, she'd almost drowned three times! That's what I call a self-destructive pattern, and luckily this is the only time I've encountered this situation. I strongly suggested that she seek professional help and recommended a therapist who also believed in reincarnation and so would understand the problem.

The young man, who sat listening to me as I brought forth his past, had once lived in Spain during the time of that infamous Inquisition. He'd been a priest but was sympathetic toward the nonconformists. And so, he would hide them and help them to escape the country and their certain death by torture. Eventually, he was caught and imprisoned. He spent five years in a very tiny cell and died a prisoner.

Although the man was born in America, he told me that he'd spent fifteen years living in Spain. By this time you know that we gravitate to the comfort of familiar surroundings, but even more significant was the fact that he was claustrophobic. He suffered from panic attacks whenever he was in a closed space.

I could go on and on recounting such events, but I'm sure you've got the idea. We are creatures of habit even in our sub-conscious thinking, and it's definitely a past life inherited condition.

CHAPTER 7

Fame

The Ballerina

Well, dear reader, I hope the former chapter provided you with a bigger picture regarding all the intricate details of reincarnation and has given you clues as to why you are the person you are today. So, just for a change of pace, I'm going to cover a couple of lives of folks who were once famous. Apart from the fun of dissecting these two past lives and how they have influenced the personalities that they are now, they are meant to show you one indisputable fact. As I mentioned in my opening statement to you, whether we're famous or not, we all have to work on baggage that we've created for ourselves. Just because one is famous doesn't mean that one gets a free pass to heaven.

Looking back over these many years and remembering the past lives I've been allowed access to, I have to say the number of famous people that have appeared have been very few. Nevertheless the two that I'll now share with you do, as always, show that every single detail of our actions is taken into consideration when it comes to perfecting our spirit. Remember what I stated earlier? People come to see me for various reasons, yet no one has ever sought my assistance because they were a famous entity in a previous life. They come to see me for the same reason as everyone does—because they are seeking answers to enigmatic situations in their present existence. Being famous or infamous in a previous incarnation is incidental, except in the way it's now affecting that individual's present actions. When it gets down to the nitty-gritty, being a famous star in the limelight is immaterial to the overall plan of life.

· · ● ● ● ● ● · ·

I met Tim and Dianna during the early 2000s, shortly after they had celebrated the opening of their shop. Since my initial visit, the place had settled into a quiet and peaceful routine with a steady flow of regular customers, and I loved spending time at their place. The building used to be a house that was built in 1922, and I'll give you its ghostly history in another story.

The room I was using for readings was on the second floor. Steep stairs led up to a narrow hallway and into a room with a sloping roof. This suggested that it had once been an attic. It was a snug room with mandalas hanging on the walls and candles reflecting their light onto sparkling crystals that sat on small tables. Incense had been burned in the room, and an odor of Patchouli still lingered.

I'd just taken a coffee break and was salivating over the remnants of a delicious cream filled donut, when I heard footsteps climbing the stairs. Quickly shaking my skirt over a trash can to discard remnants of crumbs, I wiped my face with a napkin in case cream was still clinging to my mouth.

Looking up, I was surprised to see two women enter the room. I'd expected only one person, but thought that the client had brought a friend along as a companion. This happened frequently, as it was quite common for a client to bring someone for moral support, but I soon found out that this time was different. The client asked if her friend could also have a reading .As it happened, the following time slot was vacant, so I could accommodate the second woman.

They looked to be roughly twenty years apart in age. The younger one was petite, with fine, shoulder-length hair and she was smiling with eager anticipation. The other woman looked to be in her late-fifties, with gray hair cut short in an attractive no-nonsense style. She was the unexpected client. As I invited them to sit, I noticed that the older woman was staring at me with thinly disguised skepticism. I had a distinct feeling that she was reluctant to be here, and a thought came to me that maybe the younger woman had persuaded her companion to see me. It also crossed my mind that her appearance in my room might be more than coincidence. The fact that the time slot was available was a rarity, as usually the appointments were back-to-back with no vacancies. Was she meant to be here? Because of the woman's notable skepticism, I couldn't believe that she'd come to see me of her own accord! *This woman is going to be a challenge,* I thought, but I love a challenge and recognized something in her that I admired. She probably didn't take things on faith alone. She'd want proof. The woman's attitude was the same as that of my own heart!

The young girl decided to be the first to have a reading, and frankly, I don't remember anything about her past life because the older woman's reading proved to be anything but forgettable

Whether she was skeptical or not, she was here because she needed to be and as it turned out, we were both in for a big surprise.

As soon as I entered my special space in the ethers, I saw a young teenager practicing ballet movements in what appeared to be a dance studio. The girl was pirouetting and leaping as gracefully as a seagull riding the wind. Her concentration was so perfect that she made the most difficult ballet moves look easy, and the grace and rhythm of her movements were flawless. The girl was captivating, and it was obvious that the dance was her world . . .

The doubting woman was this teenager. In this former life, she was born in Russia at the turn of the nineteenth century.

I knew that this girl was a born dancer. From early childhood, she danced the ballet and practiced until her toes bled, but the pain and exertion didn't bother her one bit. She was so focused on the ballet that throughout her life, she eliminated everything else. Nothing was as important as the dance, and she was like a horse wearing blinders so that the animal would have to travel in one direction. Her complete concentration produced tunnel vision that stopped her from seeing anything else but the ballet. It was obvious to me that the rest of this young girl's world just didn't exist. In any event, her dedication eventually paid off. As an adult, she became such a well-known ballerina that audiences would flock for miles to see her dance. It didn't matter what ballet was being performed as long as this ballerina was its star. I tried to see this Russian dancer's name, but all I could get was the letter P . . .

The reading eventually ended and as I returned to the present, I waited to see if any of it had registered with the woman. I was certainly curious to learn if she was still skeptical. Nobody said anything, but the younger girl's face held a look of self-satisfaction.

The disbelieving attitude of the grey-haired woman had changed. Her piercing eyes held mine in an intent gaze as she said, "I want you to listen to my feet when I bend them."

As she made this statement, she curled the tips of her shoes, alternately arching and bending the feet as far as she could. Even though she wore sturdy leather flats, I could hear her bones crackle as loud as firecrackers. "I've always had problems with my feet," she said. "They are tender and constantly ache."

There was of course much more to this reading than discovering why she'd returned with this physical problem. I told her as tactfully as I could that she needed to take off the blinders and see everything around her, rather than looking at the world through a narrow, straightforward vision. The message was obvious to me, but I didn't know how to politely tell her that she had a narrow-minded outlook on life. She had tunnel vision and the woman needed to know that everything in life was not black and white. There were beautiful colors to appreciate and rainbows to lighten her life. She needed to explore beyond the boundaries of her limited focus; begin to appreciate all of life and not only that which she chose to see. Her painful feet were trying to tell her that she needed to appreciate every experience as she walked her road; to explore all the beautiful scenery as she travelled the highways, instead of speeding like a roadrunner in pursuit of heaven knows what! The woman needed to look beyond the floodlights of her personal stage and mingle with the audience.

As they left the room, I hoped that the woman's young companion knew her well enough to tell her the truth without offending her.

The following day, I logged into my computer and found an email from this woman. It was almost as long as War and Peace! She started by making the following statement:

"I hope you don't think I'm being grandiose." She continued to tell me that she'd found out who she was in that former life. She had searched the Internet for information regarding Russian ballerinas of the 1920s, and wrote, "I found out that I was Anna Pavlova."

Cold chills hit me. YES!

The woman continued to give me details of this famous ballerina's life that validated what I'd seen in her past. It was obvious that she was no longer a skeptic as her words sounded so absolute. Then, she provided the clincher:

"Besides all that, I was born in this life on the same date as Anna Pavlova."

This woman, who had needed a lot of validation, had received more than she'd bargained for. Apart from other similarities that had convinced her, the same birthdates was her stamp of certification. Once again, the universal forces had being working overtime to accommodate the woman's skepticism.

The one thing that stayed in my thoughts was this: would the woman get the message from this past life, or would she be so wrapped up in having been someone famous, she'd miss the lesson she needed to learn? From my experience, some clients will only see what they want to see, but all I can do is deliver the message. That person must be willing to open up to the message, digest it, and resolve their karmic lesson.

• • • ● ● ● ● •

The Actress

The woman introduced herself as Dora. She came to my home with a friend, but as in the situation of the woman who was the famous ballerina, I don't remember the reading that I gave to her companion. Dora's was so fascinating. As with all of the past lives I've been privy to see, this one allowed me to go behind the scenes and into the thought processes of the individual as they played out their life. In the case of a famous person, this was particularly helpful as I was allowed to see details that were not recorded in their biographies.

Dora was a short, pleasingly plump woman and looked to be middle-aged. She wasn't particularly good-looking but had a personable, self- confident manner that drew immediate attention. Although she lacked physical beauty, her personality was most attractive and her warm friendliness made me feel good. She chatted with me as intimately as if I were her oldest friend. Having been raised in the British culture of conservatism, I find this outgoing American characteristic delightful, and Dora was the epitome of this grace. Some minutes of chit-chat ensued, and then I got down to the business of why she was seeing me, so here goes:

Immediately on entering her past, a sense of gaiety and camaraderie enfolded me and I felt light-hearted. The feeling increased as my sub-conscious took me back to the tail end of the 1800s. I found myself in London, England, and the reign of the elderly Queen Victoria was almost over. The scene confronting me was one of genteel frivolity . . .

A huge dining room lit with massive chandeliers hanging from a high ceiling came into focus. Their brilliance shone onto a variety of wine glasses lining either side of a long dining table. Silver cutlery and fine china dinnerware were placed in settings for the diners who sat shoulder-to-shoulder around it, while elaborate serving dishes holding various food items sat in the center of the table.

The crème-de-la-crème of London society sat at the table; women flirting with the men and the men gallantly responding. The women seemed to be trying to outdo each other in their rich and flamboyant gowns of bright colors that were enhanced by costly jewelry, while the men wore very proper black tuxedos and stiff collared white shirts ...

My inner camera stopped its perusal and closed in to settle its focus on the guest of honor. It landed on the Prince of Wales, Queen Victoria's oldest son, and heir to the throne. He was conversing with a beautiful woman seated next to him. Her name was Lillie Langtry.

Among all the attractive women at this dinner party, Lillie Langtry stood out as the most glamorous woman in London. Even the overhead lights of the chandeliers seemed to be paying homage to her beauty. As a well-known actress of the London Theater and a prominent social butterfly, she was considered one of England's most gorgeous women. She probably could have been a model for the Venus-de- Milo. People flocked to her theater performances not just to enjoy her acting prowess, but to see her beauty and bask in her personality ...

Let me digress for a moment, my friend, as you may not be aware of Lillie Langtry's fame. Maybe I need to fill you in as to the tale of Lillie Langtry and her association with the Prince of Wales. Queen Victoria reigned for sixty-four years so that the Prince of Wales was in his sixties when he became Edward VII. He only reigned for nine years before he too died. During his adult years, he wasn't allowed to take on any of the necessary duties normally performed by England's royal heirs. This situation came about because his mother, the Queen, ruled the roost and did not believe anyone else could do her job. She was a real prima-donna and always remained in charge. Queen Victoria had nine children, Prince Edward being her first born. Her private diaries were recently discovered and displayed for public viewing in the British newspapers. According to the contents of these diaries, she admits to having thoroughly enjoyed sex with her adored spouse Albert, but she didn't enjoy being pregnant. She also didn't like being a mother. So, if any of you have seen the PBS series *Victoria* don't believe the scenes that portray her as cuddling and caring for her children. She tolerated her young children, as long as they obeyed her wishes, and this attitude carried on into their adulthood.

The result of her domination over her eldest son, the Prince of Wales, was to leave him waiting not so patiently to take over his role as king. Needless to say, he had nothing else to do but fill his time with amusements. And, his chief amusement was to dally with women. Even though he was married, he enjoyed other ladies' company and had several affairs, including one with Winston Churchill's mother, Jennie Churchill. Lillie Langtry was a serious affair, and she became his mistress. Although they were lovers for three years only, they stayed friends for the rest of their lives.

So, let's get back to Dora. By this time, you've no doubt guessed that she had been Lillie Langtry in that lifetime.

During this journey into Lillie Langtry's life and her relationship with the prince, I saw them as not only being drawn to each other by the physical chemistry between them, but they had a strong intellectual attraction that was an even thicker bond. They were completely compatible and complemented each other's personalities. If you've ever been in a relationship where you and your partner knew what the other was going to say before they said it, that's the kind of close connection that these two people enjoyed. I suspect they had been with each other before this famous encounter because they were what modern society calls soul mates. I also believe that this trip back in time for Dora wasn't so much a lesson to learn but a validation of why she is the person she is today.

I could tell that Dora was absolutely delighted with this revelation. And I have to say that I too, felt a sense of well-being at experiencing such an exuberant couple who had the good fortune to enjoy a life of fulfillment with each other, even if only for a moment in time. Yes, he was an adulterer and a womanizer and yes, she had affairs with other men, but this one special relationship was one that many people hope for and never attain.

As Dora and I talked afterward, she shared with me that her present life had followed a similar pattern to her life as Lillie. I don't mean that she'd been a mistress to many different men. However, she had been married four times and also had other male friendships, but she did make a confession.

"I always said that my first husband was my prince and always will be."

My personal feelings concerning her many marriages are the result of that former life. In that life in which she had no doubt flaunted her numerous affairs, she must have had twinges of guilt for having played it out in such a promiscuous way. Remember, she lived in the era of strict moral codes, and just because she could get away with her dalliances because of her fame and fortune, it didn't make it all right in the eyes of the people or the Church of England. And so, returning as Dora, she probably felt that she had to marry her lovers because she'd returned with the sub-conscious guilt of having committed so-called sin in that former life. She now felt that she had to be proper in the eyes of her world. When I posed this suggestion to Dora, she agreed with me.

A few days after she'd left, she called me, and we had a long conversation. She had researched Lillie Langtry on the Internet (what would we do without the Internet) and couldn't wait to tell me all the coincidences she had found between her present personality and that of Lillie Langtry. That former life seemed to have dictated her present.

"I was born in California but have traveled and lived in five different states," she proclaimed.

Lillie Langtry traveled extensively as an actress, and although she was British by birth, she eventually settled in California. She loved America and became an American citizen.

Lillie had an illegitimate child she named Jeanne Marie. The child was born in March.

Dora's middle name is Jean, and she was born in March.

Lillie raised thoroughbred horses and enjoyed attending horse races.

Dora's favorite pastime is attending horse races.

She told me, "As a child, I always dreamed of becoming a famous actress or singer or dancer but never had the opportunity. As the eldest child and as soon as I was old enough to work, I had to help in their support. I've always supported myself financially, even though I had supportive husbands." As she finished this statement, she gleefully declared, "Now I know I have already been famous!"

It also struck me that maybe in this life she had been poor and worked hard to support herself and her siblings, because as Lillie Langtry, she had not experienced deprivation. Apparently, Lillie Langtry had never known what is was to be poor, and although she no doubt worked hard at her profession, she enjoyed the accolades it brought into her life. Balance is always the key in life.

Dora shared many other similarities with Lillie, including that the actress never did housework and didn't like to cook; however, Lillie could afford plenty of servants to perform these chores. Although Dora isn't rich, she made the claim that since 1972, she's employed women who have cleaned for her. She also pays for a gardener. "I don't like housework, and I don't like cooking."

What more can I say? Delving into reincarnation can be fun and in some respects, downright stimulating!

Dora's story is one of those reincarnation discoveries that let the person know why they have a certain personality and why their life is going the way it is. Whatever lesson Dora may need to learn from it was not made clear to me, but she did say that knowing of this past life had certainly enhanced her present. It is one of those validations that I've often seen and in this case happened to be a famous life.

Dora is one of those people who have kept in touch with me over the years and has become one of those clients that I call "shirt-tail friends." Like that ship that passes in the night, she periodically stops and toots her horn at me.

She recently let me know that she's moved to a new house and has given it a name. She calls her new home "Lillie's Pad."

CHAPTER 8

Ghost Stories

The Haunting

You may be asking yourself what ghosts have to do with reincarnation. Well, even though the following events I'm going to share with you didn't directly involve past lives, the line between the world of so-called ghosts and a spirit returning to the body is sometimes blurred. What I mean by this is that following the death of a person, there's a period of rest that is a time to rejuvenate between incarnations. And, as always, I don't take this theory on faith alone. I've had a few incidences whereby I've been made aware of this condition. It's what I call a time of recuperation. For want of better words, I think of this state as being a no man's land, where entities are recovering from a former life before once again entering the earth plane. And my feeling is that occasionally these waiting entities show up as so-called ghosts. I don't pretend to know why they feel a need to make a ghostly appearance. It could be that they're reluctant to leave that which has been familiar to them, or they're not yet aware that they've left their body. This latter condition sometimes happens after a physical death has been instantaneous. There have been many books written covering these phenomena so I leave it to you to seek them out, if the subject interests you. I do however emphasize that my own theories are only my personal belief. It is a fact though that for whatever reason, ghosts do make appearances. Once again, I'll give you a personal incident that can explain better than I can.

The ghostly visitation happened to involve my friend Fran—the person who had talked me into attending that dream circle when I was still living in Phoenix. Many years after that occasion, and long after I'd moved to Oregon, I paid her a visit. By this time, Fran had purchased a new home in the northern end of the city. Rapid growth had taken place since I had lived there, and where once had been a vast desert covered in sage brush and giant Saguaro cactus, there now stood wall-to-wall houses, condominiums, shopping malls, car lots, and etcetera. My friend's new home was in a sprawling sub-division.

After a day spent catching up with each other's lives, and making myself comfortable in her new home, we eventually sat relaxing in her cozy living room, sipping on mugs of steaming coffee and snacking on junk food. During a lull in our conversation and out of the blue, she declared, "I need you to use your psychic expertise for me!"

I didn't say anything, waiting for her to deliver an explanation.

"I have a ghost haunting this house."

Well, this unexpected announcement surprised me, as the house wasn't the type of place that ghosts usually haunted. After all, it was brand new and very modern in its design—not at all old and decrepit.

So . . . what's happening?" I asked.

She told her tale. Apparently she'd been lying in bed one night, but not yet asleep. Her bed room door was ajar, and all at once she saw the fleeting shadow of a man run past the doorway. Being as my friend is at times impulsive and definitely foolhardy, she got out of bed to investigate. She turned on every light in the house, but it was empty.

"Sometimes, when I'm sitting on the couch, watching TV or reading, I feel someone standing behind me."

"So what do you want me to do?"

"I want you to make him leave!"

I'm sure you've already gathered that I don't waste my time on saying no to any requests Fran makes as she doesn't know the meaning of the word. Besides, I have to admit that my usual fascination with the paranormal needed to be indulged. And so, I prepared to listen to any information that my Head Honchos deemed to be pertinent.

Taking a last sip of the delicious coffee and placing the empty mug on the coffee table, I cleared my mind of outside interference, tuned in to the right station, and went with the flow . . .

Immediately a tall Indian man, wearing the Indian costume of bygone days, stood in front of me, and he looked very angry. I mentally asked him why he was feeling so upset. It turns out that he's the former occupant of the land that the house is now built on. The whole area of this sub division had been an Indian encampment, and his teepee sat where my friend's house was now standing. She was an intruder in his home and he wanted her to leave!

As delicately as possible, I mentally explained to him that his tribe's land no longer existed. His tepee was gone. As gently as I could, I told him that he was stuck in the wrong century and needed to move on toward the Light as he no longer occupied a human body . . . After a few more minutes of mentally sharing a conversation with him, his image disappeared . . .

My friend is no longer haunted.

• • • • ● ● • •

The old House

Around the beginning of this new century, I spent a weekend giving readings at Tim and Dianne's previously mentioned metaphysical store. The shop had wonderful energy within its walls because of its original use as an early twentieth century home. Consequently, it's had plenty of time to become potent from the energy of its former inhabitants. And it was full of ghosts, but they weren't nasty ghosts.

Tim and Dianna are delightful owners who had lovingly converted this home into its present format, and I felt uplifted every time I entered the place. The warmth didn't emanate just from this couple; it was in the bricks and mortar of this former home.

The first time I stepped across its threshold, I was instantaneously met with the ghosts of former tenants and visitors. I saw groups of people clad in the style of the 1920s. These ghosts stood in groups as if having the pleasure of chit-chatting with each other. They seemed to be present to celebrate the opening of this store and were thoroughly enjoying themselves. The party atmosphere was stimulating, and it seeped into every space in the shop, so that it enfolded me as I entered.

Tim shared an experience with me that had sent him scurrying out of the building. He was doing most of the renovations to convert the house into its present business format, and on one particular day was in the act of demolishing a wall of the stairwell. As his hammer hit into this wall and made a big hole in the plaster, he saw a book that had been hidden behind it. Full of curiosity, he reached inside the hole and removed it and on closer inspection, realized that it was an old family Bible. How it had got behind the wall is anybody's guess but feeling excited, he opened it to its front page. Like most old Bibles, the first page recorded the births and deaths of the family who had originally lived in the house. Tim couldn't wait to take it home and show it to Dianna, and when he did, they decided to keep it.

When he returned to the business of renovating the place, spooky things began to happen. At first he ignored them, but the strange happenings, such as lights turning on and off without any physical cause, continued to get his attention. No, it was not faulty electrical wiring. The ghosts became more insistent in their spooky haunting, and Tim was becoming increasingly nervous. So, after one particular eerie event, he hurriedly packed up and went home. He told Dianna that they needed to return the Bible to where it belonged, which they did. The disturbing haunting stopped.

Were the ghosts of the family who had owned the Bible upset with Tim for having disturbed its hiding place? Who knows? As Shakespeare said, there are stranger things in heaven than on earth—or something similar to that.

• ◦ ◉ ● ● ● • •

Lifting the Veil

What I'm now about to tell you is without any doubt, proof that there is no such thing as death. The event I'm about to disclose is way beyond the veil of our known reality and is something much more controlled and powerful than human life.

Once again, it took place at Tim and Dianne's store. This particular weekend, I had given a Friday night talk on reincarnation and was now following it with two days of requested past life readings. Saturday morning I arrived early, just as the store opened for the day. The first thing I did was to look at the client list to see what time the first person was to appear.

People always made an appointment in advance and would leave their name, phone number, and the date they'd made the appointment. Naturally, this information was necessary in case there was any change to the schedule, or anything unforeseen happened.

A woman named Sandy was at the top of the list and due to arrive at ten o'clock. Tim was minding the store, and we stood idly chatting as I waited for her arrival. We weren't too concerned when ten minutes past the hour had arrived and she hadn't shown up, although being late wasn't a good idea as I tried to stagger the appointments so that they wouldn't overlap. For this reason, a fifteen minute break was allowed between appointments so it wasn't a real problem—yet. By ten-twenty I was getting nervous. Could she have been in an accident?

The bell over the top of the door tinkled as it was pushed open, and we both looked toward it in expectation. A woman walked in and approached the counter.

She spoke to Tim. "Do you have anyone here who gives past life readings?"

We turned and looked at each other in astonishment and the same thought passed through both our minds. The woman obviously wasn't Sandy, but was this a coincidence? Sandy hadn't shown up, but this woman who had no appointment, had!

I made a suggestion to Tim. "Why don't you call Sandy and see what has happened? Maybe she forgot that she had an appointment. Meanwhile, seeing that I'm free, I'll take care of this lady's request."

The woman followed me up the stairs to my room, and after I'd completed her reading, she left. Returning to the main floor, I approached the front desk where Tim was standing. He looked almost comatose!

"What's wrong? Did you get hold of Sandy?"

"You're not going to believe what's just happened." Tim's normal self-composure seemed shaken, and I wondered if the ghosts had been playing tricks with him again. He began an account that sounded so ludicrous that my first thought was that he'd lost his marbles!

Sandy still hadn't made an appearance, so Tim had called the number she'd left on the schedule list. After a few rings, the phone's answering machine picked up, so Tim left a message. A few minutes later, the store's phone rang.

Tim answered, and a man's perturbed-sounding voice spoke. "I don't know who you are or what the devil you're talking about, but you just called my cell phone and I live in Oklahoma."

I forgot to mention that this metaphysical store is in the state of Washington, halfway across the country from Oklahoma.

Tim explained to the man that he was the owner of a store in Washington and told the details of Sandy's broken appointment. He apologized, stating that maybe she'd given the wrong number to call. They both hung up.

A few minutes later, the phone rang again. It was the same man from Oklahoma. "What did you say that woman's name was?"

"Sandy."

There was a heavy silence from the other end of the phone. The man finally spoke. "That was my wife's name, but she died a year ago."

Do ghosts have a psychic link that allows them to operate modern technology, such as cell phones? Tim wanted me to call the man back, but I declined. I felt that Sandy had accomplished what she'd intended, so it wasn't necessary.

My thoughts were that the man was no doubt still grieving, and this was Sandy's way of letting him know that she was still with him. She may have left her physical body, but her spirit still stayed around him. I played with the notion that maybe her spirit had tried to contact him before this, and she was unsuccessful as he was so grief stricken, he was blind to anything else. Or, it may have been a situation whereby he didn't believe in the supernatural, and therefore when she attempted to contact him, he blocked the connection. For whatever reason, Sandy had used Tim's spiritual place and me as a channel to communicate with her husband. It was her attempt to bring him solace. Tim and I had served her purpose. Nothing else needed to be done.

We discussed this incident with Dianne and the other two people who worked in the store. No one remembered having taken down that particular appointment. Then Tim made a startling discovery. Once more, he looked at the schedule list. It showed that Sandy had made this appointment in <u>March</u>. This particular weekend event didn't take place until the following <u>May</u>. The rest of the people had not booked appointments until April, as the date selected for my weekend event was not decided upon until mid-April. Tim and I had not had any communication during the month of March.

As always, spirit does not leave any loose threads. Another person had been provided to fill Sandy's appointment so that my time wouldn't be wasted.

What can I say except to once again repeat myself? We may have a free will to choose our own journey but ultimately, the Universal Force is always in control.

CHAPTER 9

Angel In Grubby Blue Jeans

The angel that saved my life was originally included as a part of my first book (no longer in print) called *God Walks and Talks.* The incident took place during the mid- 1990s and was such a dangerous situation that under normal circumstances it could have at the minimum, caused serious injury and at the worst, killed me. Here again, this account doesn't exactly comply with the subject of reincarnation, but once again, it is undeniable proof that Divine Will steps in when our free will is seriously out of control. It's like watching a young toddler as they explore their new surroundings. While you may allow the child the freedom to examine their world, you will quickly intervene when you see that they're about to harm themselves. You don't let them place a hand on a hot stove.

For this reason, dear reader, I feel that it's even more appropriate to share this story with you now, than when originally published. I'll explain what I mean.

Because of the tremendous and chaotic challenges we're facing in today's world and the resulting high stress level, it's a perfect time to let you know that your guardian angels are always around to protect you. They are on the job twenty-four by seven. And the tremendous imbalances and fear expressed in our present world make it very necessary for you know that you're safe. You need validation that you are not without help when you're blindly trying to navigate the pitfalls and perils you are presently encountering in our world.

Yes, we return again and again to fulfill our karmic destiny and yes, we do have free will to follow a chosen path, but my dear friend, your own personal angels are a constant and protective force. There is a time we are born and a time we die, but when it isn't our time to leave but we're teetering on the edge of a precipice, our personal protectors inevitably pull us back to safety.

My angel in disguise confirmed this.

I should have taken a different road. For the hundredth time, I mentally kicked myself as once more I slammed my foot on the brakes to avoid hitting the rear end of the car that was mere inches in front of me. For the past thirty minutes, I'd struggled to drive out of Portland's jammed city center streets onto this major highway that would take me home, not expecting to get stuck in snarled traffic. *Why was I so stupid as to take this route on this night of all nights?* My anger and frustration were mounting rapidly as I mentally chastised myself. Of course, I should have remembered that this was the night that the basketball team was playing at their home stadium and it was their next to last game of the season.

The Portland Trailblazers were in contention for the NBA championship. They had won this night's game and their final one for the coveted prize was to be against the Los Angeles Lakers. Over the past year, fans had become increasingly excited, and the stadium was packed to full capacity at every game. Tonight had been the climax.

I'd attended a meeting in the city center and unfortunately had left just as the game was ending. As I'd left the parking facility and entered the busy street, I was met with vehicular insanity! Hundreds of cars were trying to make their way home by every downtown road available. Aggressive drivers were in frenzy; honking horns and slamming on brakes as they maneuvered their way through the city. After weaving my way through the mess, I'd eventually reached this major highway that led to my home in a Westside suburb. I'd breathed a sigh of relief, thinking that I now had it made. Wrong!

A few yards into the highway, a flashing warning light had indicated that the left lane (the fastest) was closed. Although there were no workers on the highway at this late hour, the lane was still blocked off. Why? There was no machinery sitting in the lane and no dangerous holes, so why was it still closed? My tolerance for the city's road workers' seeming stupidity was nil!

A cement median divides this six-lane highway into three for east bound and three for west bound traffic, and it's the fastest route for people going in and out of Portland's city center. If the closed lane had been open, the amount of extra traffic would not have been any worse than at rush hour, but with only the middle and right hand lanes available, it was bumper to bumper and stop and go. This particular highway is a bear to drive at the best of times. It curves around the base of a mountain range, and there are sharp curves to maneuver. Cars travelling west have to make a steady, uphill climb as well as having to control the drive around those sharp curves.

Those city workers probably closed off the lane because they knew that tonight I'd be driving this way! I was becoming irrational. Once more, I hit the brakes as the car ahead of me stopped again. The next exit ramp was miles ahead, so leaving the road wasn't an option. Besides, I was stuck in the middle lane with no room to move over, so even if there had been an exit ramp, I couldn't have reached it. There was nothing to do but crawl along like a crippled snail, blindly following the line of creeping traffic.

Stress continued to rise in sync with the hill I was climbing. The glare from the headlights of the east bound traffic coming down the hill hit the windshield with blinding force as vehicles whizzed past. Accidents on this highway were frequent as folks rarely obeyed the fifty-five mile speed limit, unless a cop was around. Most cars hit sixty five or seventy as they sped around the curves. Even semi-trucks broke the law.

My car had standard transmission, so I was trying to keep my foot from riding the clutch as the car crept along, but being on a hill it was difficult to do, as I was afraid it might stall and roll into the car following me. Meanwhile, that idiot behind me insisted on riding my bumper. I could see his face in my rearview mirror and he was glaring at me as if this problem was my entire fault! To use the emergency brake wasn't feasible under the circumstances. For the hundredth time, I wished that I'd left earlier instead of chit-chatting after the meeting. *Better still, I shouldn't have attended. Period!*

The asphalt writhing upwards in front of me seemed as if it were a slinking black serpent. The tail lights of cars in front of mine blinked on and off as we all tromped through the night. *Will this never end?* Cars continued to limp forward and upward like the movements of a Conga line of dancers. Deda-deda-da-bump-bump!

AT LAST! After three miles of climbing, I saw a wondrous sight! A few yards ahead I could see that the third lane was finally open. As the cars further ahead of mine reached the open lane, they were swerving into it and speeded up like jets taking off from a runway. Traffic began to thin out as the extra lane relieved the pressure, and I breathed easier as I anticipated reaching that open lane and heading home.

What I'd failed to notice during my preoccupation with the driving conditions was an odd smell inside my vehicle. That smell was now getting stronger. As I drew nearer to the open third lane, I prepared to gather speed and clamped my foot down hard on the accelerator. Nothing happened. I pushed the gas pedal and at the same time attempted to shift gears. There was still no response—except for a loud, protesting roar of the engine. Once more, the foot came down as I tried to change gears. The engine whined in protest, and the clutch sank all the way to the floorboard. It felt like a wet sponge underneath my foot. *Oh, no!* I slapped the side of my head as my brain finally registered a truth. The clutch had gone kaput. I cussed loudly in English as well as American. Here I was, stuck in the middle lane of this crazy highway and couldn't budge. I tried to control my rising panic, but still had enough sense to turn on my hazard lights. Not only was I stuck in the middle of racing traffic, but was also sitting just around a bend of the mountain. Cars couldn't see me until they came around that bend and were practically on top of me. *I'm a sitting duck.* Approaching cars were already careening to either side of my stalled car as the newly opened lane allowed them to gather speed.

You're probably thinking that the logical thing to do would be to get out of the car and push it to the side of the road, right? Naturally, that thought occurred to me—quickly followed by the realization that if I should leave the car in the middle of this mass of speeding traffic, I would probably get hit. I'd be playing Russian roulette. It would be akin to suicide, and being as I'm a devout coward, I wasn't quite ready to meet my Maker.

Plenty of horns blasted at me, as drivers swerved to either side of the stalled car, but nobody stopped to help. Would you believe that one driver gave me the finger as he swerved to avoid hitting me? I felt like a Thanksgiving turkey waiting for the chopping knife. *Where are the cops when they are needed?* I alternately cursed and prayed for help as I sat grasping the steering wheel as if it were a lifeline.

"Can I help you?"

I jumped out of my skin! A gentle tapping on my driver's side window accompanied the inquiry, and a young man's face was pressed against the glass, peering at me. He looked very concerned underneath what looked like a two-day growth of whiskers covering his jaw.

Rolling down the window, I answered, "My clutch has died and I can't move the car. I'm stuck."

"Do you have a flashlight?"

"No." I felt helpless as well as stupid.

He straightened up from his bent position. "Wait a minute, I'll be right back." He turned away and made his way across the left lane toward the median.

To my amazement, I saw that there were no cars within sight of the fast lane as he strolled across. It was then that my eyes landed on a bright yellow Volkswagen bug sitting by the side of the median. *I wonder how it got there without my seeing him drive up and park.* As he reached the Volkswagen, he opened the rear door and bent over to look inside, as if searching for something, and then I couldn't help but notice that he wore dirty-looking jeans that looked as old as Levi himself. He wore no jacket over a thin T-shirt, even though the night was chilly. *Maybe he just got off work.* Then, I silently slapped myself for being critical. *What do you want girl, a man dressed in a tux, ready to take you partying?* "My brain was still addled.

He apparently found what he was looking for and straightening up, closed the door and turned to walk back to me. It was then that I saw what he was holding. He was carrying a big lantern; the kind that hunters or miners use. *Why did he ask me if I had a flashlight when he already has a more powerful light?*

Once again he was at the side of my car. "I want you to release the brake, and then turn the wheel toward the shoulder." He pointed toward the right hand side of the road. "Let your car roll backward down the hill; at the same time keep turning the wheel in the direction of that shoulder. I'll walk behind you and direct the traffic away from the car as you steer it across the lanes."

With these words, he turned from the window and walked to the rear of the car. As nonchalantly as if he were taking a stroll through a park, he swung the huge lamp high in the air to alert oncoming traffic, while beckoning with his other arm for me to follow his direction. Keeping my eyes glued to the rear window and the swinging lamp, I gingerly eased my foot off the brake and allowed the car to slide backward. As I slowly turned the wheel and steered the car across the highway toward the safety of the shoulder, I deliberately refused to look at the on-coming traffic. This stranger who was guiding me was forming a protective barrier between me and the deadly, racing motorists, and that's what I concentrated on.

Holding my breath as I let the car roll backwards, I glued my eyes on the powerful beam of light that spewed forth from the lamp held in his upraised hand. It reminded me of the shepherd that was guided by the light of the star to Bethlehem.

Walking across the road swinging the lantern, he motioned a semi-truck to slow down as my car started to slide across its path. It was hurtling right at us, and I almost wet my pants! Transfixed, I watched dumbly as the huge rig barreled toward us—then at the last minute it swung sharply out of our path as easily and as swift as a bird in flight. My body trembled uncontrollably and my grip was frozen to the wheel, but I was safe. I'm not of the Catholic faith, but I silently murmured a few Hail Mary's and some eastern Ohms for good measure.

It seemed like hours before we got to the safety of the shoulder but eventually did and came to a halt. Relaxing my grip on the wheel, my body slumped into the seat as deflated as a burst balloon. I don't know how the feat had been accomplished without my "savior" not getting killed, but it had. Vehicles had miraculously avoided him as he'd walked across the mad-dashing highway.

The tension in my body was palpable, and I couldn't stop shaking. My stomach was in knots and feeling slightly nauseous, I leaned my head out of the window and gulped in air, at the same time planning to get out of the car as soon as my legs would hold me. I needed to thank my rescuer, who was standing quietly at the back of my car. At that same moment the flashing lights of a police car pulled up behind me. *Now a cop shows up*, I thought sarcastically.

The young man approached the squad car as the officer rolled down his window and leaned his head out in a questioning manner. I couldn't hear their conversation but sat and watched through my side-view mirror as they talked. After a minute or two, the policeman got out of his car and approached my driver's side door. My rescuer remained by the police car.

"Do you have triple A?" he asked.

I acknowledged that I did and fishing in my wallet, took out my AAA card.

"Good." The policeman held out his hand to take the card from me. "I'll call a tow truck driver from my radio and have him take you and your car home."

Turning around, he headed back to his car, and I too turned my head toward the spot where my young man was standing—but the spot was empty.

Taken aback, I looked across the still busy highway to where his Volkswagen was sitting by the median. There was no Volkswagen. The space was empty.

Dumbstruck, I leaned my head out of the window to search up the hill for a yellow bug that was possibly climbing among the traffic. The bright lights of cars lit up the roadway ahead and competed with the highway's iridescent lights, but no yellow Volkswagen was in sight. My eyes once more searched the place where his car should have been sitting. The median that divided the lanes was there in all its concrete glory, but it didn't shelter a yellow Volkswagen.

I could see quite plainly for about a quarter of a mile up the hill, and the car couldn't have disappeared that fast. Shaking my head in bewilderment, I sat contemplating what had just taken place. It couldn't have been more than a few seconds that the young man had stepped back to allow the cop to come over and talk to me. *Nobody y could disappear that quickly!* But he had.

Still shaken, I opened my door, got out, and leaned against it for support. The police officer was still talking on his radiophone. Shading my eyes against the glare of headlights, I once again scanned the steeply rising highway in front of me, still not believing that he could have left that fast. Even more incredulous was the fact that within a short space of time, and without getting hit by traffic, he'd walked across three lanes of a very busy highway to his car. He had then apparently got into his car and driven away. It was impossible. At the reckless speed that cars were driving along this road, he'd have been hit before reaching his car. *There is no way he could have done it.*

However am I going to be able to thank him? I didn't know his name or anything else about him. I knew absolutely nothing about a person who had risked his own life to take control of mine and guided me to safety. I didn't want to think of what might have happened to me if he hadn't come to my rescue. Underneath that dark, bristly beard, his face had shown so much kindness and concern for me.

"A tow truck will be here in about ten minutes." The policeman had returned to my side and said he'd stay until it arrived.

My befuddled mind was in such a whirl that it didn't enter my head to ask this officer if he'd gained any pertinent information from my Good Samaritan.

Cars and semis continued to flow past like an army of robots going into battle, unconcerned and uncaring. Later, I would kick myself over and over again for neglecting to ask the cop for any personal information the young man may have provided.

Had my helper really been there? . . .

* * * * * * * *

"I'm telling you, it was humanly impossible" The look of skepticism on my friend's face irritated me. "Don't look at me as if I'm nuts! At least I would have seen his car, even if I had missed seeing him weave across that highway amidst vehicles that could have killed him! I'm telling you, he was an angel in disguise."

Carol tried not to show the amusement and disbelief she was feeling. "Sometimes, you carry your paranormal ideas too far. The next thing you'll be telling me is that he wore a cape with a big letter S for Superman on his shirt. He sounds more like a skid row bum than an angel."

I shut my mouth. There was no way I was going to convince my down-to-earth friend that I was right in my belief.

Carol heard the frustration in my voice, and I could tell that she felt uncomfortable for being sarcastic toward me. She sounded placating as she said, "There's probably a logical explanation for his reluctance to stick around. Maybe he had no car insurance and was afraid that the cop would find out. Or he may have a bunch of unpaid traffic tickets that he wanted to keep hidden. Some folks are pretty irresponsible, you know."

"You can scoff if you want to," I retorted. "I know you don't believe in guardian angels and my metaphysical theories. I know you think it's all a bunch of New Age hogwash. You may be right, and I understand your logic, but tell me this, if you're so smart. If he's such an irresponsible person who drives without insurance and collects unpaid traffic tickets, how do you explain his responsibility toward a perfect stranger? For heaven's sake, he placed his own life in jeopardy! There were hundreds of cars that passed me and didn't stop to help, and one driver even gave me the finger as he passed for causing more problems for him! And how could he get across that highway amidst all that traffic without getting hit, then get into his car and disappear so fast? How do you explain that?"

Carol remained silent. She had no logical explanation to give.

CHAPTER 10

Two Different Worlds

W hat I'm now about to disclose may blow your mind, but it does depend on your current thinking. By this time, I'm guessing that you've allowed new vistas to open that have taken you beyond the limitations of our known world. And whether you will think that the facts about to be revealed are ridiculous and a product of my imagination or you'll have the satisfaction of having another viewpoint validated is entirely up to you. It depends solely on your present mindset. But regardless, the following events occurred exactly as described.

Andrew

Now, before starting Andrew's story, I'll introduce it with a conversation that I once had with a twelve-year-old granddaughter.

Tammy has always been a precocious individual, and one never knows what she's going to say next, or how her brain works. She's now a young woman and still has a mind of her own; always saying what she thinks, in spite of what the reaction will be from other people. Anyway, this twelve-year-old was in the back seat of my car as I drove her home after a visit with me. Tammy and I were talking back-and-forth as the car sped along the highway, when out of the clear blue sky, she posed an unexpected question.

"Nana, do you believe in aliens?"

The car almost slid off the road! *Where did that come from?* Straightening the steering wheel, I digested her question and answered in the only way I knew how.

"Well, Tammy, we would have to be pretty egotistical if we thought we were the only life form in this vast universe that's full of other galaxies and planets besides ours."

"You are so right!" Her childish voice was full of triumph as she continued. "Even if there is only a tiny atom of life on another planet, it's still a life."

Only twelve years old, and she was having such far-out thoughts. I was floored. Later, I told her mother about this conversation, and she told me that Tammy had been watching the popular TV program *Ancient Aliens.*

• • • ● ● ● ● •

The first time I encountered an alien from another world wasn't Andrew, but I'll tell his story as his reason for being here was so dynamic. When he came to see me for a reading and his past appeared, I was just as astounded as I'd been by Tammy's question.

Before I continue though, I need to clarify that these other worldly meetings are not a common occurrence. I can count less than five fingers as to the number of clients I've seen that have come here from another dimension. Even so, just as in the case of those two clients whom had lived as the famous actress and ballerina, these aliens remain unforgettable. Besides this, these outer-space encounters have really broadened my perspective as to the utter vastness of our universe. I might add that these encounters have also left me feeling envious of their superior knowledge.

When I was first approached by one of these so-called aliens for a reading, my immediate thought was that if they are so advanced that they know how to travel from their dimension to ours, why would they need to seek answers to their existence from a mere human being? A logical question right? Since humans have barely explored outer space, let alone traveled to another galaxy, why would they consider our inferior knowledge to be worthy? Well, in the case of my own contacts with them, I have learned that these visitors are here for different reasons than those for which we humans incarnate. Pretty soon, you'll see what I mean and the reason why they sought my attention.

By the way, if you are wondering what these outer space visitors looked like, they didn't look like little grey men with buggy eyes and they were not the least bit frightening. They looked like you and me.

For instance, Andrew was a handsome man who looked to be in his late forties or early fifties. His dark brown hair was slightly wavy, and he sported a thick, dark mustache. As he sat opposite me waiting for me to begin, I was reminded of a young Tom Selleck. Yes, he was that good looking. His air of charming self-confidence was also very appealing.

And so, this unaccustomed event began:

This is odd. What's going on? My alternate self had entered another galaxy that was way out in the endless universe, and my sub-conscious camera was concentrating on a planet situated far from our earth. This unknown planet seemed to dominate a vast area amidst strange-looking nebulae. My conscious mind wanted to discard the image, but needless to say, the sub-conscious was in control; besides which and in spite of this unsettling feeling, my curiosity was aroused. To be bluntly honest, if I were a boozer, I would have blamed this situation on the result of having consumed too much alcohol! Still, the longer this image stayed, the more I felt a creeping sense of calmness and peace come over me. I'd never felt anything like it before and changed my mind about wanting to get rid of the scene. In fact, the longer this peaceful feeling stayed with me, the more I found myself wanting to stay in this unknown space. The word serene took on a whole new meaning.

As I floated in this strange realm and continued to view the planet, its image became more pronounced and a name appeared in the picture. Although

I instinctively knew it was the name of this world, I couldn't decipher it. The letters were not of any earthly language, and the spelling of the name completely flummoxed me. Still, my heightened senses knew intuitively of its importance in the universe. This world was honored and its name respected.

My other self slowly drifted toward this place and eventually landed on its surface. I could now see the inhabitants. Although the forms appeared to be similar to human form, they were much taller and much more slender. Their images seemed to be almost translucent and would fade in and out, continuing to disappear and return as if they were shadows. To my conscious self, these actions seemed reminiscent of human lungs, breathing in air, then exhaling . . .

My Head Honchos informed me that they were a far more highly developed race than humans. I then became aware that they were communicating with each other via mental telepathy and was given the impression that they were so high in the evolutionary stage of life that speaking was unnecessary, although they were capable of speech . . .

The only way I can describe their civilization is that it was like the Biblical description of the Garden of Eden. They had no wars, no disease, and no dangers of volcanoes erupting or terrible hurricanes that caused floods. There weren't any of the earth-shattering catastrophes that we experience. Perfect peace reigned, and it was what we call a place of paradise . . .

I also knew that the Tom Selleck look-alike sitting in the room across from me was originally from this planet.

As soon as the knowledge of this man's existence came to me, the scene changed and focused on one of the planet's occupants. Of course it was Andrew in his former life, and I felt the personality of this alien entity.

I was told that he'd been very complacent in his former life on this planet, almost to the point of laziness. He took his lifestyle for granted and felt no gratitude for the fact that he lived in a place of such ideal conditions. This entity was selfish and thought that he deserved this life of ease, and any concern for the welfare of others never entered his head. Ironically, it struck me that he was mimicking humanity's base traits.

The punishment for his laxity was thus. His superiors told him, "You don't appreciate your life here, so you have to go and live on planet Earth and experience what it's like to feel pain."

My mental reaction to these words was that even in a perfect world, one still has to pay the piper when one indulges in bad behavior …

After I'd received enough information for Andrew to comprehend his past existence and for him to recognize why he was here, I felt myself returning to my own reality. I was very reluctant to leave such a peaceful and ideal place …

Still in a state of euphoria, I slowly came back to earth. I opened my eyes—and was dismayed at the sight that greeted me. The man sitting in front of me was crying uncontrollably. This handsome man who had seemed so full of self-confidence was quietly sobbing like a child.

Feeling very uncomfortable at witnessing Andrew's distress I remained silent, waiting for him to regain his composure. After a few moments he was able to control his emotions and the crying stopped. Then after a brief pause, he started to share his personal life with me.

"I've always felt like I didn't belong here," he said. "It's hard to describe, but I feel that there is something better for me and my spirit is constantly yearning to find itself. I feel disembodied and lost. I'm always so lonely."

He continued in this vein in a voice filled with despair, and shared many painful experiences that he'd endured throughout his life. His devastation was obvious.

Although I explained the reason as to why he was here, it really wasn't necessary. Andrew already knew. I was just the catalyst that had forced him to face the truth. It was now up to him whether or not he was going to do the necessary work before he could return to his home.

Later, via an accidental conversation (ah) with someone who knew him, I learned that even though he'd shared a lot of personal information with me, he had not disclosed the fact that he was in the middle of a nasty and painful divorce. It was also his second divorce.

Andrew was here to digest the full impact of a pain that he'd never felt during his life on his home planet. As always, Universal Law doesn't mess around when teaching a lesson. He had to know what it felt like to be unloved and to experience heartbreak.

• • • ● • ● • • •

Future of Earth

Although the following event happened many years ago, long before my meeting with Andrew, it has stayed in my memory as clear as if it happened yesterday.

It took place at one of those monthly psychic fairs that I once participated in at Mark's metaphysical store.

The woman who entered my room looked much older than the majority of the people who crossed my path. It was hard to guess her age, but she looked to be in her late sixties or she could have been seventy. She was a little person, probably no more than five feet, two inches, and as she sat down in the client's chair, she exuded such an air of ease and contentment that I asked myself why she was seeking a reading. Most clients display a sense of curiosity, or in extreme cases, their body language shows a certain amount of anxiety. This woman seemed to be so complacent and her energy was so relaxing, that it felt as if I were being given a massage!

As I began to leave the store's surroundings, a creeping sense of tranquility spread through me that seemed like an extension of this woman's energy. Maybe it was the same sensation that some of the astronauts seem to take on while in outer space. I knew I was leaving Earth's atmosphere and the further I went, the more complete the silence became…

I found myself drifting higher and higher into outer space, and when I came to a halt, saw our planet lying below. Its image was like one of those spectacular pictures that the astronauts sent back when they first landed on the moon. So awesome! But perusing its surface from this out-of-body perspective, I started to realize that even though it was our planet, its geography had changed. Whereas once there had been landmass, now there was water. The seas and oceans of earth covered places where continents and islands had stood; big cities and rural villages where people had once resided were gone. In fact, whole sections of our known world had disappeared.

Yet, the biggest shock came when it was revealed to me that I wasn't seeing a past timeline; I was being given a glimpse of the future! I was being shown our Earth as it will be in the twenty-third century. This had never happened before and has never happened since. Feelings of excitement overcame me as I mentally thanked my guides for allowing me this unique privilege.

Earth's geography had definitely altered. Because of climate changes and consequent melting of icebergs, the seas had risen and taken over the land. Inevitably, this condition had caused a major problem for humanity. There was no longer enough land left for people to occupy and the planet was suffering from overcrowded conditions …

Then, I became aware that my sub-conscious was showing me this older woman as she would be living in that future century, and although she resembled the old lady, she was very much younger. She would be known as a "Facilitator"….

Once again, I was floating above our planet, but this time I wasn't too far from the realms of our earthly atmosphere. And a scene appeared that looked like something out of a science-fiction movie. Unfortunately, our known vocabulary is too limited to be able to fully describe what I was seeing, but I'll do my best . . .

I was being shown futuristic, steel-and-glass buildings that appeared to be suspended in clusters in outer space. I can only describe the scene as being similar to a present day suburb. Yet, these buildings were of strange-looking shapes and designs that I'd never seen in any suburbia of today. They were suspended together far above Earth, but still remained in our galaxy and were composed of brilliant, architectural designs. The only way I can describe these buildings was that they looked like something from the Star Wars movies. But these future buildings were even more sophisticated and bizarre looking than any science-fiction movie. There were newfangled living accommodations that, in comparison, made our present homes look like medieval shacks. Although I was given only one suburb to concentrate my sight on, I got the strong impression that this was one of hundreds of such places scattered throughout outer space . . .

Then my sub- conscious switched me back to earth. My alternate self became focused on a scene that was taking place during this future century. I saw people standing in long lines, as if they were waiting for stores to open on Black Friday—except this wasn't a line of bargain hunters. They were waiting to be taken to these outer space suburbs. These people were immigrating because they could no longer survive on Earth due to its present condition. It was not their choice but a necessity. The scene was similar to a present day airport terminal as folks stood in line, waiting to check-in for their flight. But instead of the airport that we are accustomed to, with numbered gates that direct you to various terminals depending on where you are going, the people I saw were at designated spacecraft terminals. This future "airport" was much more sophisticated than Cape Canaveral as folks waited to board streamlined spacecraft that would transport them to their new homes far away from earth . . .

This whole scenario was too incredulous for me to describe adequately, and I realize that as I now write this, it must seem to you to be beyond the bounds of reason. My friend, I can understand this thinking, as it felt this way to me. However this is one of those times when you need to think "outside of the box." We are already feeling the effects of climate change. And, it is my belief that at this present time we're only touching the tip of the iceberg, when it comes to the ramification of this problem. Also, who knows what kind of accomplishments mankind can perform in future centuries? We've already gone beyond exploring the moon. What's next?

As my focus was returned to the Facilitator, I was told that her job was to educate these departing emigrants on how to use artificial oxygen in their outer space environment. They would need oxygen to survive in their new communities.

Wow! Of course, they would! I was shocked and so completely wrapped up in a sense of awe at seeing the future that it hadn't dawned on me that humans need oxygen to survive. I couldn't see how this oxygen was supplied, but was given a sense of its mechanism. The only way I can explain its set-up in our present world's limited terms and my ignorance of modern technology is that it reminded me of unseen, centrally located power grids that directly supplied all the buildings without the residents having to fiddle with individual units and thermostats . . .

When this realization was given to me, my logic kicked in and common-sense told me that they'd need more than just a small oxygen tank, and they certainly couldn't run around their new homes wearing cumbersome astronaut contraptions.

As with Andrew's planet, I wanted to explore more of that future world but was told that it was time to return to the present. I'd been given all that I had to see for this woman's needs. After all, it was her future, not mine . . .

Unwillingly returning to the present timeline, I reentered the room in the shop. Even my surroundings seemed antiquated! I sat staring at the elderly lady, feeling uneasy. *Is she going to think I'm a fruitcake?*

"So, what do you think? Could this have possibly made any sense to you?" I asked.

Giving me a very direct look, she calmly replied, "I've always believed in UFOs."

She was completely unperturbed by my revelations of her future life.

I don't know what the lady was supposed to learn from this information for a future life, but having been given the privilege of seeing it I can hazard a guess. I believe that in this life she is being prepared for this future incarnation. Also, she was probably being reassured that she was on the right road to her destination. I felt it was something she already instinctively knew, but for whatever reason, she needed a reminder. It also crossed my mind that being allowed to see this future earth was a wonderful gift to me. As I'm a typical Capricorn with Saturn's sometimes dour rule, it gave me a sense of positivity for the future of humanity rather than seeing the chaos in our present world that sometimes fills me with doom and gloom. Whenever I view all the negative news on TV or the Internet, I remember this experience, and it lifts my morale. I'm reminded of humanity's tenacity and resilience.

You may be interested to know that sometime after this event, I was reading one of Edgar Casey's books and came across an item that told of one of this psychic's predictions. He said that he'd seen the future of America and that Nebraska would become a seaport. He also said that most of the West Coast would no longer exist. His prediction did not say when this would take place, but my own eyes show me that it's already started.

A few months after giving the woman her future reading, she called and asked if I would give her another. As I'm usually reluctant to do a second one

I hesitated to say yes, but in the case of this lady my curiosity got the better of me.

The second life I saw was also a verification that she apparently needed. It also told me why she believed in UFOs.

As in the case of Andrew's incarnation on our planet, it was revealed that she too was originally from another galaxy, and her people were far more advanced than we are. However, unlike Andrew, her lesson was not to learn pain but to rectify a karmic mistake her people had once created here on our Earth.* Her job in this life and also in that future life was to help humanities spiritual progress in any way that she could. Thousands of years past, the people from her planet had visited us and due to an error in their judgment, they had interfered in the natural progression of our development. It was payback time.

I was allowed to see this lady's persona when living on her home planet. As clear as a sunny day, I saw her as a man who appeared to be seven feet tall. His body was exotic and beautiful; light olive-skinned with fine-boned features that seemed to be a cross between a Mayan Indian and an Egyptian. He wore a type of loincloth similar to the Native American clothing. The most interesting feature were several, elaborate gold chains around his neck. I was told that they denoted his status as a leader; similar to a military officer who wears decorations to denote his rank and experience.

Incidentally, I was also informed that this little lady was only one of thousands of people from her home planet that were here to help correct the problems that humanity is experiencing.

I realize that these concepts may seem far-fetched to some people, and unbelievers will no doubt think me whacko. But after seeing so many unexpected and intricate events in the past lives of humans, I've learned that

---

* Should you be interested in learning more about the planet that this client was from, read *Genesis Revisited* by Zacharia Sitchin.

anything is possible in the universe. And humanity does not have a monopoly over our universe. We're only one spoke in the grand wheel of life, and from having been given these experiences of other life-forms I'm convinced that we're not even a major spoke in that wheel!

CHAPTER 11

Relationships

During the early 1950s there was a popular song recorded by that great vocalist Frank Sinatra called *Love and Marriage*. One of the lines went as follows: "You can't have one without the other." Are you old enough to remember it? It doesn't matter if you're not, as it only entered my head because of that particular line. That one line perfectly describes the connection between reincarnation and relationships. I know we now live in an age where being wed isn't a precursor to co-habituating, but whether you are legally married or living with a mate, that line still aptly describes any and all relationships. And the tie between reincarnation and life is akin to being Siamese twins. Even surgical separation can't break that special bond. It's the same situation between people who are strangers to us—we are all indelibly connected.

My friend, if there is nothing else that you've learned so far, I hope you've learned that the main reason we reincarnate is to work on perfecting our spirit. And the way in which we accomplish this is through human interactions. As the saying goes, "The teacher learns from the student" as well as vice-versa and the interactions we have with each other are either an opportunity to grow, or not. Eventually, if we've done the necessary work and enhanced our spirituality to the highest degree, we can return unblemished to our Soul Source. I know it's a long and hard trek toward reaching that goal, but it's the primary reason we've continued to return for millennia.

The following stories I'm about to relate are two instances of negative relationships versus positive. How we conduct ourselves in a relationship always determines whether or not our journey is going to be smooth or rough. The outcome of any relationship with another person (or persons) is that we either move toward our goal or make a mistake and have to correct that mistake before we can move on. As you will soon see, these two stories are as extreme in their outcome as one can possibly get in this world. The people involved are prime specimens of course and effect.

So let's start by dissecting these two personalities via the most significant of relationships—those between lovers.

Example number one:

I used to have a friend who was an intelligent, attractive woman and had made it to the top of her profession. She was highly respected for her work ethics and skills and admired by her peers. She was also lots of fun to be around—that is, when she wasn't in the middle of a crisis with her latest love entanglement.

As far as her work environment was concerned she had it all together, but her relationships with the opposite sex was a different story. When it came to choosing men to share her life, she was as short-sighted as a cross-eyed mule who doesn't know his right from his left. Her personal life was a continual merry-go-round; hopping on and off the ride and never stopping.

This friend married her first husband at the age of nineteen and soon had two children, a boy and a girl.

Her husband should have gone to jail, but didn't, after it was discovered that he was molesting their fourteen-year-old daughter. It blew my mind when she shared this story with me—and still does. Instead, when his sexual perversion was revealed, the child welfare authorities stepped in and gave my friend an ultimatum: either she leaves her husband, or they would remove her children from this toxic environment. Believe it or not, she chose to stay with her husband, and the children were taken into foster care.

Eventually she did come to her senses and divorced the man.

When I asked her why she had married him, she answered "Because he wouldn't leave me alone, and when I went away to college, he followed me, so I gave in and married him."

Sometime after obtaining this divorce, she remarried.

At the time that she and I met, she had recently divorced this second man, but they remained friends. I met him and found him to be both good-looking and very charming. Naturally, when she'd married him she thought he could do no wrong, and I admit that he presented himself to me in a very good light, although I did think him to be a bit too suave.

After they had been married for a few months, he quit his job because, he told her, "I'm sick of having to wear a tie to work every day!"

Incidentally he also had two teenagers from a former marriage, and they lived with them. By this time, her own children were once more living with her and consequently, she became the only breadwinner for six people.

She spent several years in this situation while supporting this lazy you-know-what before she had saved enough money that she could leave him and start over again. Oh, by the way, the reason she had no money was that when they married, she sold her home (at his persuasion) and poured all the money she'd gained from its sale into remodeling and making major, needed repairs to his house.

I've now lost touch with this former friend because I had to break the connection. Her energy was so negative, she depleted mine, and although I felt sad, I knew I couldn't continue this detrimental friendship. Whenever we would meet, or talk via the phone, I'd have to listen to her latest, heavy-duty drama that she was playing out with her newest male friend. It was always the same play but with a different man. The relationships were always emotionally abusive. After having to listen to her latest disaster, I'd feel drained, and if I attempted to give advice, she'd interrupt, completely ignoring my interjections. All she wanted to do was to cry on my shoulder.

The last time I saw her she was still searching for another man to marry and still dating losers.

You don't need to return again and again to learn a lesson. I'm sure that having come this far in reading this missive, you've no doubt found out that you are given ample opportunity to ace the lesson in this life. You know that the same scenario will repeat over and over again until it gets your attention. Without any doubt, this is what was happening to this former friend. But eventually the human body wears out and whether you get the message or not, you have to give up—until you return anew.

At this point, you are probably thinking the same as I am; that is what will it take for this woman to come to her senses and get the message? She had everything going for her; an excellent job with financial security, attractive appearance and nice personality, yet no common sense when it came to her choices of male relationships. Sadly, if she doesn't get it this time she'll probably need to be hit with a two-by-four to get her attention! To say that she has a problem with intimacy is an understatement. But whatever psychological reasons she has for inflicting such trauma on herself, it's for sure that she'll once more fall off that ladder she's trying to climb and have to mend those broken rungs before she begins to climb again.

Her life is a good example of trying to drive through a dead-end road and continually hitting a brick wall.

Think of this planet that you inhabit as your school. Those teachers you have are all the relationships that you participate in and how you handle the intimacy of these connections depends on your own actions. That's why it behooves you to heed those gut feelings when you're about to make a mistake.

Before making a major decision, listen to your angels, Higher Self, or whatever you believe to be your guidance. You can choose to either act or react, and that in turn may become either a positive or a negative. It all depends on your decisions. Therefore, my friend, when the teacher is trying to teach you, it's a good idea to pay attention.

• • • ● ● ● ● • •

The following story is an entirely opposite situation, although similar in its basic relationship; the bond between a man and a woman.

Example number two:

This friend I truly miss, as she passed over all too soon. But I really value the few years that we were able to spend together as she taught me the meaning of endurance.

She was born with displaced hips, and the problem wasn't discovered until she was seven years old. Can you believe that her parents didn't know that something was wrong before so much time had passed? I once asked her how she had learned to walk with such a handicap, and her answer was, "Because I was expected to do so."

After her condition was diagnosed, she was placed in a hospital, underwent numerous surgeries, and spent a year in a body cast. Even so, the doctors told her parents that by the time she reached the age of forty, their child would be in a wheelchair.

We first met when she was fifty-odd years old. At that time, she was walking with the aid of a cane and suffered chronic pain, but she never used a wheelchair.

To add to this challenge, she was raised by a mother who suffered from the disease of alcoholism, and whenever she became intoxicated, she would abuse the child. This mother would knock her to the floor, continue the abuse, and refer to her as a hopeless cripple. As my friend related this story to me, I wondered why the father hadn't stopped the abuse. She told me that the father was so wrapped up in himself, he was emotionally unavailable. Apparently, he was totally blind to his wife's cruel behavior.

This friend married at eighteen. She eloped with her spouse after having known him for one month. They stayed married until her death some forty-odd years later. She and her husband had a happy life together and managed to have one child. Not only was the bond with her husband strong, but the mother-and-son relationship was also very close. It was obvious to anyone that knew them that they truly had a loving family relationship.

Despite her physical handicap, her home was always immaculate and made me ashamed of my own sloppy housekeeping. She crocheted and embroidered beautiful things and made me a gorgeous artificial-flower arrangement in an antique urn. It's kept in a place that can be seen by anyone entering my home. She was always busy and volunteered for various organizations that helped to care for less fortunate people. Folks depended on her for her steadfast support, and because of her upbeat attitude, they seemed to forget that she was handicapped—that is until one saw her face turn pale from the pain she was feeling. She relied on round-the-clock medication to control this pain, but didn't abuse the drugs.

These two extremely opposite relationships are examples of how we resolve the challenges (or don't) that come into our lives. The lives of these former friends are stark illustrations of how our free will can direct our decisions in either a good or not-so-good way, especially in such an intimate relationship as that between lovers. Do we have to return once more and do it all over again, or do we hit a 100 percent on the test and move up to a higher level of growth?

Let's take a look at another intimate relationship; the relationship with our parents. Maybe you were raised by loving parents in a secure environment and grew into an emotionally stable adult. Instead, you may have been born into a dysfunctional family, such as my deceased friend experienced. This latter situation could either leave you with a low self-esteem, or you have risen above it and become stronger from having learned from such negative conditions.

My belief in reincarnation follows the notion that we choose our parents before we are born in order to accomplish a certain lesson we need to learn. Therefore, you might ask why we would deliberately choose to enter an abusive family unit. Could there be something really dynamic from a former incarnation that we have to resolve? One simple possibility is that we choose an abusive relationship because we're reversing a role. Maybe we were an abuser in a former lifetime and need to suffer for what we've inflicted on someone else. Does this sound far-fetched and too simplistic? Think about it for a moment. How can we understand what pain is if we've never felt it? It's like a person who says "I know how you feel," when they've never experienced a painful loss. Think on Andrew's condition. Even though he came from a perfect world, for his own sake he needed to feel the devastation of pain. Is the emotion of pain a part of the learning process?

On a positive note, it's a possibility that my handicapped friend with an abusive mother may never have cultivated her hidden talents if she had been physically fit and in a secure family environment. The challenges she had to face could have broken her will. Instead, she chose to become stronger. On the other hand, and for whatever psychological reasons, the other friend flunked life's challenges—big time! Why? Was she repeating a negative pattern that she'd previously cultivated in a former life, or—as in the case of the other friend—had her childhood also been abusive? If either scenario is true, had she chosen to allow the situation to affect her emotional growth instead of pulling herself up by her own bootstraps?

While writing my book *Dreams Mirrors of Your Soul*, I asked people to be a part of it by sharing their dreams with me. One woman said she dreamed she was sitting in a classroom, and the teacher was writing on the blackboard. He wrote: "All That Matters Is Love." It's that simple. But we humans seem to want to make it almost impossible to love one another. Wouldn't the world be so much nicer if hate didn't exist? Why would we have to keep on returning if our relationships were like Adam and Eve before she plucked that pesky apple and got kicked out of that garden?

That diamond of various carats has so many different facets to it that those relationships that determine the outcome of our karmic destiny take many forms

Let's take this one step further. When we incarnate, we are here to resolve all the gamut of human emotions. Every aspect of the psyche is considered, and nothing is left undone. Your life isn't a black-and-white photograph. It's a portrait that's created by a divine artist.

That pilot that died in a blazing fire and his anger at being senselessly killed before his time returned with a double, emotional whammy. He not only returned with a fear of fire, his anger had also returned with him so that it negatively impacted his relationship with his family. Outcome: these emotions had returned with him as a part of his psyche and were affecting his capacity to have a fearless life and a loving relationship.

The impulsive and tactless King Edward's Lady of the Court had rein-carnated with that rash personality of yore. She was egotistical, which prob-ably was (once more) affecting her dealings with her husband's political career. There's nothing wrong with having an ego. We wouldn't have an ego if we weren't meant to. It's when we become egotistical that we're in trouble. Outcome: she'd returned with that same, rash personality trait.

Why do we return with physical, mental, or emotional incapacities that affect our relationships with friends, family, or co-workers? It's all a part of having to do a good job so that we can get a perfect score and return home. Simply put, dear reader, it's what is known as karma.

I agree with psychologists who believe that we are preconditioned into feelings of inadequacy. We can certainly recognize a problem we've created in our current environment because it's tangible, but it's much harder if the preconditioning has manifested from a previous lifetime, because it sits in our sub-conscious memories. Fortunately, in this day and age, there are professional counselors who also believe in reincarnation, so naturally they will (and do) help.

There's an excellent book dealing with this very situation called *Many Lives, Many Masters* by Brian Weiss, MD. I highly recommend it as an example of preconditioning from a former life.

On the other hand, do we choose to carry a so-called handicap to enhance our spiritual development? Think about it. Let me use that famous person Ray Charles as an example. Did his blindness enhance his musical abilities? Would he have developed this wonderful gift if he had not had this handicap? Would he have enjoyed such worldwide relationships if he had his sight? Would he have developed his musical gift if he could have read the notes and seen the piano keys?

Biggest question—did he choose this handicap to jump-start his spiritual growth? There are a lot of questions to mull over when attempting to decipher the intricate psychology of reincarnation.

I could continue in this vein forever if I had all the answers to life's relationships and how they affect our past and future lives, but I don't. But what I have learned from the glimpses I've been given of the past in relationship to this life is enough to keep me busy for many lifetimes! Maybe I'll leave the final answers to that Divine Psychologist known by many names, and for now, I'll concentrate on the relationships I have now. I'll try to engage in them with positivity and loving energy in the hope that this attitude gets me out of this present life without getting me into too much trouble! I recommend that you do the same.

CHAPTER 12

Namaste

I honor the place in you in which the entire universe dwells.

I honor the place in you, which is of love, of truth, of light, and of peace.

When you are in that place in you, and I am in that place in me, we are One.

Sanskrit. Interpretation. Beth Paris.

And so, dear reader, I've come to the end of this epistle. If I've helped to expand the boundaries of your existence, then I've accomplished my goal, which is to assist you in a wondrous and meaningful life. My hope is that something I've written has resonated with you, such as an incident that you might have puzzled over that now makes sense. If this is the case, then I've served a purpose. Maybe you feel a sense of completion after absorbing this read, and being an avid book worm myself, I know that feeling when you turn to the last page and feel satisfied, even though you're sorry that it's ended. Should you too feel this way, then I'm humbly grateful that my contribution has given you this pleasure. If the entire above conditions are true, you are now ready to move on to a broader perspective of who you are and your purpose here on this earth. In the East, it's called enlightenment.

But if you still have unanswered questions, maybe at least I've planted a seed so that you will be urged to find the answers in other ways. Perhaps you will be led to an event—possibly another book, such as the ones I've already suggested by Brian Weiss and/or Zacharia Sitchin. Or it might be a casual conversation that you'll engage in with someone that will turn on a light switch for you, giving you the answer you need.

The most important thing for you to do now, my friend, is to trust that everything in your life is going according to plan. Even if you are puzzled by a situation you are in, or an event that seems odd, trust your inner guidance, better known as your gut instincts. Trust really is a magic word.

Should you unfortunately be experiencing a painful situation in your life, again let it go and hand it over to your divinity. Your helpers are always willing to work things out for you. How do I know this? They sent that angel to save my life, didn't they? Most of all you need to be kind to yourself when a difficult experience enters your life. We all make mistakes, and there's a reason why you're tripping over rocks, or driving over roads full of potholes. It could be that your life is out of balance and the rough road is a reminder that you need to be more grounded. Are you operating from an egotistical position or are you being mindful?

Just to recap: remember that even though you do have free will to choose your own road, your angel guides are always willing to assist you in making the right choice. All you have to do is ask. Maybe that choice you've made is the wrong one, and that road is more difficult than you had anticipated. As I've already told you but will reiterate—it makes no difference as long as you keep in mind that mistakes are also an opportunity to learn. So, think about it—is it really a mistake? Regardless of your choices, you'll get to where you're supposed to be in your own good time.

Remember that "mistake" I made when I attended that dream interpretation group and was given the opportunity to take a big step forward? In my ignorance, I turned down that opportunity offered to me and failed to expand my knowledge. As the saying goes, "You can lead a horse to a trough, but you can't make it drink." I'm the first to admit that when the powers that be opened that door for me, I was a real horse's you-know-what! No matter; although I took a longer and more difficult route to get to where I was supposed to be, I eventually found the right road and the doors were flung wide open. In retrospect I know that I wasn't ready to move forward at that specific time. When I was ready, I was once again given the opportunity.

The point is that regardless of how many wrong turns you make and how many times you hesitate to step into unknown territory, you will accomplish what you set out to do. If you miss the boat you're meant to board, don't worry. Another one will sail into your harbor to pick you up and carry you to your destination.

Luckily, if we ignore an opportunity to expand our spirituality, we're always given another chance—and another—and another. The only effort we have to make in order to move forward is to be willing to take one step at a time.

I'd like to put this question to you. Have you ever considered that we may return because we simply enjoy being here? Is there any other place in our universe where we can indulge in the pleasures of being human?

Just take a moment to think about the following: spirit isn't matter, it's ethereal. And, because we're in the confines of this body, we have a tendency to forget this. When you visualize someone who has died, don't you automatically think of them in their physical form? We may still feel that person's energy and visualize them in a body, but because of our limited, earthly thinking, most of us can't see their spirit.

So, does our spirit sometimes want to return just to have the experience of being in human form?

Most folks take their five senses for granted, but I ask you to give a thought as to how you would function without them. Would we be able to enjoy relationships with other people? Do you remember a moment in your life when you first encountered someone who completely bowled you over? What was your reaction? If it was a relationship that promised romance, you probably felt the chemistry that flowed between yourself and that person, right? At that special moment, we feel a sense of expectation and excitement. The taste and touch of lips meeting in a kiss is exhilarating. You can smell their skin and see the same joy as yours in their eyes. My friend, you are using your God-given human senses.

At the opposite end of the spectrum, we use our senses when we are in a "fight or flight" situation. But I'm not thinking of a life-threatening situation, although our senses do kick in and are on high alert at such times. I'm posing a situation when we may find ourselves in the presence of an obnoxious person. What if you're at a party and introduced to someone who is offensive. Maybe they lack personal hygiene, or are drunk, or their laughter is too loud as they try to be the center of attention. They display an egotistical persona . . . I'm sure you've run into a similar occasion your life. Do your five senses come into play? Of course they do! You react accordingly, and if you can get away from their presence, you do so.

Our senses are an absolute necessity, and I wonder if extra-terrestrials from other worlds have the same advantage? Once again, I'll use Andrew, the alien from another planet as an example. He was, for the very first time, feeling pain! Does that perfect world "out there" lack the senses that we take for granted? Is this a reason why we sometimes choose to return to have the experience of feeling?

Most people are in such a hurry to cram as much activity as possible in twenty-four hours that they don't take time to actually enjoy living in our world. Modern technology does have its advantages, but it's sucked us into believing that we need more than twenty-four hours in a single day in order to exist! It's called instant gratification.

Recently, a friend and I were sitting in a restaurant, and an elderly couple sat at a table a few feet away. They were already seated as we were led to our table, but were still waiting to be served their meals. I noticed that they were using their cell phones and continued to be absorbed in them as their food arrived. From the moment that we entered the restaurant until we left, this couple didn't say one word to each other! They were too busy playing with their phones and still concentrating on them as they ate. They could have been eating cardboard as far as their interest in their food was concerned.

Are we living a life as non-communicative robots?

Slow down. Turn off your phone, your electronic devices . . . get out of social media and relax in the moment! Get to know yourself.

I used to be one of the biggest sinners with a road-runner attitude. When I was working, there were many times that I'd exist on coffee instead of eating because I didn't have time to take a break, to sit down and relax.

Among all the mayhem and crisis in our world, there is much beauty to see and it just might be possible that we return here to appreciate this beautiful planet. Use all your senses with eyes to see the beauty in sunsets, ears to hear the cry of a newborn baby or laughter of a child. Use your olfactory nerves to smell the fresh air of an ocean beach, or taste the salty tang of that ocean spray as you wade into an oncoming wave. Stop and hug a tree and experience the sense of strength its rough bark gives you. Use all your senses to get the full impact of living. Life is a gift, dear reader, so live it to its utmost.

Anne Frank said it best when she said, "In spite of everything, I still believe in the goodness of man." In spite of all the seemingly uncontrollable mayhem we've created in our world, we are still pure at a soul level.

Would you like to know what I do in my retirement? Each morning, I sit on my porch with my coffee, and really soak up my surroundings. I'm fortunate to live in a country setting, so I contemplate the giant fir trees with their massive trunks. They've been here for many more years than I have, and

I wonder what tales they could tell if they could talk. They're so strong and steadfast. Storms may blow and snap off their branches, summer's heat dries the ground they're rooted in, but they stand firm and unshakable.

I listen to the doves' gentle cooing and wonder where they are, as they're not in sight. But I hear them, and that's enough pleasure. I watch the robins scurrying across the grass, looking for their breakfast, or chasing another bird into the heights of a tree. I may even be lucky enough to have a breeze come by and touch my face in a caress. And my coffee tastes so good! That's living, my friend.

Don't wait until you've retired to appreciate your world. Live each day as if it were your last. Yesterday is history and tomorrow is still unknown. Our world is still a magnificent one in spite of all the damage we humans have created. Just remember that what is happening to its inhabitants is fear-based and you can get rid of fear by trusting in your own worthiness. If we all do this, then our collective consciousness can overcome anything.

If you've learned nothing else in reading this book, you've surely learned that I always demand and honor validation. And if I've helped you to validate your own self-worth then I've done my job.

This idea may sound ludicrous, but when I talk of people incarnating because they're taking a vacation, it is a fact because I've had clients verify this. They have chosen to return to enjoy our planet because they've earned this right. Sound ridiculous? Just think of someone you know to whom nothing 'bad' ever seems to happen. I know a couple who have been married for over thirty years, and each year on their anniversary he sends her eleven roses. He sends only this number because he says that she's the twelfth rose. They've had their challenges, but nothing really tragic has happened to mar their contentment. Are folks like this taking a vacation? Has this couple found the meaning of life? They've certainly found the meaning of love.

Even though we are living in horrendous times, I know that our planet and humanity will survive. How do I know this? I've had validation, of course!

During my years of giving psychic readings, I also was given the honor of seeing a few, very special children who already know what their purpose is on Earth. These children have been called by some people "Indigo children," but their earthly name is immaterial. I prefer to think of them as angels who have earned their wings.

The first time I did a reading for one of these children, it was such an emotional shock that I had a hard time holding back tears. They are powerful old souls and their strength of spirit is unimaginable.

As always with clients, they did not come to me by accident. For approximately six months, first one mother then another came to me asking if I would give a reading for her child. This is not the norm because my logical mind tells me that children are too close to their source to need or understand reincarnation. But after a steady flow of receiving these requests, it finally sank into my thick brain that I was being directed to give the readings.

The ages of the children that came to me were between twelve and fifteen. Half a dozen of them showed up over a period of a few months, and they all had one thing in common. Not only were they very old souls, but they were so highly developed spiritually that they didn't need to be here. They had <u>volunteered</u> to come here to help clean up the mess we have made of our world. The strength of their spirits flowed from them and impacted mine with an uplifting energy that completely bowled me over. I felt honored to be in their presence. They love Earth and its inhabitants so much that they are willing to take on earthly sufferings to save our home. And what was really amazing was that when I read for these children, they already seemed to know their destiny. They showed no surprise. One of the mothers emailed me the day after I'd seen her child and said, "Whatever you did was a good thing because she cleaned up her room today!"

The mother was being facetious but was the child demonstrating her bigger job as a cleanser of this Earth?

Although we are living in a time of physical and emotional mayhem, remember, my dear friend, that your soul is indestructible

And so, on that note I will leave you with this comment that you might want to share with skeptics. Whenever anyone tells me that they don't believe in reincarnation, I give this answer. "That's okay, the next time around you will."